Nurturing Our Children To Succeed

Susan Lipper

BUDDING SELF-IMAGES, INC.

ROCKVILLE CENTRE, N.Y.

Copyright © 1999 by Susan Lipper

ISBN: 0-9674865-0-5

Library of Congress Catalog Card Number: 99-90403

All rights reserved. No part of this work may be reproduced or utilized in any form or by any means, electronic or mechanical, including photocopying, microfilm and recording, or by any information storage and retrieval system without permission in writing from the publisher.

First Printing

Printed in the United States of America

Cover design by Fernando Agudelo

For information regarding ordering, call: (516) 942-2015

A guide for helping parents and teachers understand and address the emotional and academic challenges facing our early childhood students of today.

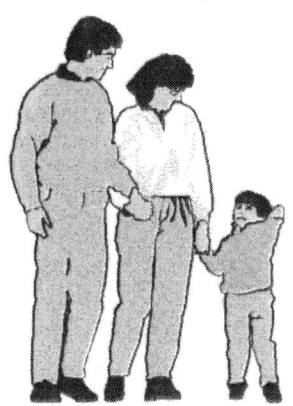

24 June 05

Dear Darris,

It was a real pleasure meeting you during the training session. I greatly appreciate all of your help, patience & kindness!! Thanks to you, I am beginning to enjoy my laptop. Wishing you all the

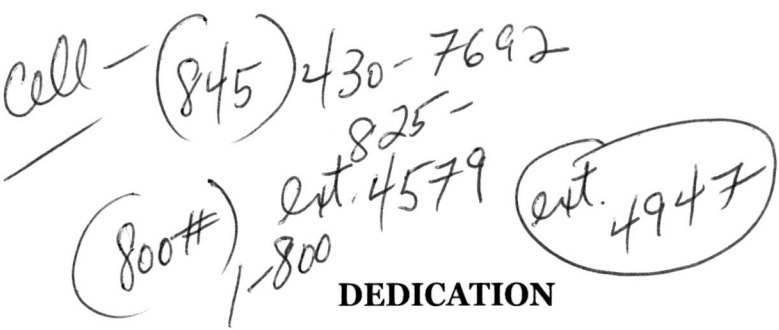

DEDICATION

To Allan - My best friend, soulmate and the love of my life.

To Geraldine - My guardian angel, who helped me mend my wings so that I could fly again.

To My Parents - Who always believed in my teaching career.

To My Students - Who inspired me every day to reach beyond the walls of the classroom to teach through love.

In Memory of the one and only **Shari Lewis**. May she forever live on in the hearts of children throughout the world.

ACKNOWLEDGMENTS

I'd like to thank my family for their love and support, especially my niece and nephews - Hillary, Benji, Robby and Ilan, for their unconditional love and affection.

Many others have helped me along the way. My dear friends Patti and Sue have always encouraged me to live my truth. My gratitude to Cecilia for always believing that one day I'd write a book.

Helene has consistently reinforced my creativity and believed in me.

I send my love and deep appreciation to Lila, Mary, Erika, and Heather. They have served as role models for me in following my dreams.

Many thanks to Chrissy and Melissa for helping to make my stay in New Paltz wonderfully productive.

My years in the classroom would not have been as fulfilling had it not been for the kindness, sensitivity and commitment of my educational assistants - Cynthia, Doris, Cecilia, Alice, Karen, Michelle, Gloria and especially Claire.

Thanks to all the parents throughout the years who were proactive in the education of their children. Their involvement made all the difference. I really appreciate the extra help of all my class mothers.

All my love and appreciation to my colleagues, especially Moe, Doris, Mary and Ivy, who always laughed with me and kept it light.

My heartfelt appreciation to Dorothy, Terri, and especially Carol who helped me get this manuscript out in such a professional manner.

I would also like to thank Fernando Agudelo for his beautiful cover design.

Lastly, this book was produced by Steve and all his associates at Sterling-Pierce. I am so grateful for their outstanding work.

AN EXPLANATION

The individuals mentioned in the case examples are composites of many of the students in crisis who I have taught during my twenty-four year career.

The experiences of children in crisis are sometimes similar. Any similarity of examples to specific individuals is only a result of these typical characteristics.

Contents

Foreword xiii

Introduction xviii

Part One
THE IMPORTANCE OF NURTURING OUR CHILDREN IN SCHOOL

CHAPTER 1
Starting First Grade As Seen
 Through The Eyes Of A Six Year Old 3

CHAPTER 2
Children in Pain Can't Always Cry 15

CHAPTER 3
A Look At Some Of My Students 29

CHAPTER 4
Creating a Learning Environment That is
 Safe For Children to Take Risks 41

CHAPTER 5
The Importance of Character Building 54

CHAPTER 6
The Need For Smaller Classes With Educational
 Assistants 63

CHAPTER 7
A Multi-Level Approach To
 Helping Our Students 69

CHAPTER 8
Establishing Healthy, Productive
 Communication Between Parent and Teacher 78

CHAPTER 9
Creating Intimacy and Fostering
  Self-Esteem Through Storytelling 86

Part Two
THE ROLE OF THE FAMILY IN HELPING OUR CHILDREN MEET SUCCESS IN SCHOOL

CHAPTER 10
The Importance of Quality Family Time 95

CHAPTER 11
Suggestions For Parents On Establishing
  Healthy Communication That Will Enhance
  Their Child's Self-Esteem 108

CHAPTER 12
READ! READ! READ! 118

CHAPTER 13
Homework Doesn't Have To
  Be A Big Struggle 126

CHAPTER 14
Informing Children About
  The Dangers In Our Society 133

CHAPTER 15
A Positive Vision For the Future 144

**Ten Steps To Nurturing
  Our Children To Succeed** 148

Need More Help Than
  Your School Can Provide? 150

Bibliography 153

FOREWORD

May this book ignite the hearts and souls of parents and teachers everywhere who will be touched by the inspiration that Ms. Lipper offers. True inspiration comes from deep within the heart. It comes from an internal knowledge of what is right and good and needed. *Nurturing Our Children To Succeed* is written from the heart. It connects the reader to a deeper understanding of what is truly taking place throughout a child's educational years.

We all recognize that children need to have responsive and loving parents. We understand that children need to be surrounded by teachers and helpers who are sensitive, both to their academic progress, as well as their emotional growth. Yet, how do we fully address our childrens' needs? Ms. Lipper enables us to reflect upon the essence of learning, and teaches us how to foster receptivity in our children. Her book offers a practical guide to help us create the nurturing environment that is necessary and essential for the blossoming of our children's hearts and minds. Through her insightful examples, she demonstrates the effectiveness of teamwork between educators, parents and children. In essence, the team effect functions as a safety net for our kids, increasing their chances for success.

By establishing a strong rapport and bond with our youngsters, we further help them to succeed. In her book, Ms. Lipper stimulates our memories of our own educational experiences, which serves to strengthen our empathic connection with our children. Only when we ourselves are able to dig deeply into our hearts for memories of our own years gone by, will we truly be better prepared to foster the development of the children of tomorrow. For many of us reflecting back on our school years, our most significant memories are often of an emotional nature. In my own personal experience, two of my most vivid memories have little to do with my academic progress, and everything to do with my internal emotional development.

Let me share with you my memories of Julie. Thinking back, she was obviously a neglected child. At the time, however, the signals must have been overlooked. It seemed that everyone involved in placing her in my first grade class must have had their fingers crossed, hoping that she would be able to adjust. That was not the case. From the beginning, the class could sense that something was not okay with Julie. Her hair was matted and tangled, her face flecked with scabs. As incident after incident occurred, it became clearer to all of us that she was truly troubled. Although I was young, and I knew that it was rude to stare, one morning during our snack time I couldn't help myself. I was curious to see what Julie was up to. She was seated in the back of the classroom and, as usual, appeared to be in a world of her own. This particular morning she was sinking her fingernails into a waxy milk container, making it rain white. She frightened me. I think she frightened the entire class. We didn't understand that type of behavior. Of all my memories of the days, weeks and years that I spent in school, I never forgot Julie's pain. Now, as a mother of two children, and a therapist in practice for eighteen years, I can only wonder what had really been going on with Julie. Looking back, I realize that no one had been able to reach her and that no one knew how.

The book you are now holding gives a practical guideline for parents and teachers, enabling them to recognize the signs of a troubled child. Ms. Lipper provides tools to help alleviate our childrens' anxieties. She helps all of us involved in a child's education to work together so that no child remains unreachable or isolated. *Nurturing Our Children To Succeed* shows us techniques we can use to build an intimate, emotional bridge to our children. In this way, our kids feel guided and protected, permitting them to love the process of learning.

How does one learn to nurture our children in a more effective manner? With few role models to emulate in many of our lives, it can be difficult. That's why Ms. Lipper's book is so significant. She provides us with tried and true examples from her own teaching career which give us ways to achieve our goals and help to ensure success! She teaches us to focus on the whole individual, addressing both the academic and emotional facets of every child. In this way, through our sensitivity and responsiveness to each child, we ensure that the Julies of the world do not slip through the cracks.

In the ten years that I have known Sue Lipper, I have seen her act as a powerful advocate for countless children, all of whom continue to love her. I have observed her in her creative classroom environment. She is a role model, an example of a giving, nurturing human being, a teacher who will never be forgotten.

It is mandatory that we learn the ABC's during our school years. Unfortunately, it is *not* mandatory that we be nurtured as individuals in the process. In *Nurturing Our Children To Succeed*, Ms. Lipper intimately shares her insights from her twenty-four years of experience as a teaching professional. Hers is a vision of a unified team, providing harmony, sensitivity and emotional security for all children.

>Geraldine Lowenherz
>Relationship Counselor
>Colorado Springs, Colorado

INTRODUCTION

The year was 1973, and I had just finished my student teaching in an inner city school. One of my most rewarding experiences was studying with a great teacher of English as a Second Language. Her enthusiasm was contagious, and the children in her classroom thrived.

Day after day she sheltered and supported them with her loving trust. Each child came alive with a love for learning. In this stimulating arena, I witnessed the girls and boys taking risks, like reciting a new English vocabulary word, phrase, or even a question.

Observing this deeply touched my heart, because I had grown up listening to my parents' stories of how difficult it was to come to the United States of America without speaking a word of English.

My mom arrived in the Upper West Side of Manhattan from Lisbon, Portugal at the age of fourteen. My dad's family settled in Forest Hills, New York from Bucharest, Roumania. He had just turned fifteen. They met at a wedding in New

York City, and shared the sad theme of how they and their parents had fled Europe after the Nazi invasion.

I was so intrigued by their stories, that I knew that this was one area of teaching that I'd love. So, you can just imagine how thrilled I was when I received my first appointment as a Teacher of English as a Second Language in Flushing, New York.

My classes were comprised of kids from various countries around the world. Each student brought with him or her the rich heritage of his native land. I could feel the energy ready to take off in the room. All I needed to do was make it safe for them. This is where I intuitively combined my knowledge of Teaching English as a Second Language, my sensitivity to how frustrating it is not to be able to understand and express oneself in a new language, with my sense of humor, patience, praise, encouragement, love of play, and willingness to share some of my own childhood vulnerabilities. Ultimately, the children became aware of the fact that I too was once a shy, often scared, student. Therefore, I was able to empathize with how they frequently felt.

My students grew to trust that I would be, first and foremost, *consistently kind*. The priority value that I set for myself was that I would never,

ever shame a child, ***for the only thing that shaming teaches is fear!*** Moreover, when a child is consumed in fear, risk taking will always cease.

> *"A slow student is not cured by sarcasm. Mental processes are not mended by mockery. Ridicule breeds hate and invites vengeance."*
>
> Ginott, 1972.

This brings to mind the touching story of a little Greek girl named Suzu. Suzu was in my first kindergarten E.S.L. class. For a very long time, words never rolled off of her lips. However, I recognized a readiness to speak in the expression in Suzu's eyes. Therefore, I had to trust that there would be a favorable outcome. For, intuitively, I strongly believed that any day Suzu would utter her first English words. Sure enough, my theory was proven to be correct. This is what happened.

One morning I was demonstrating picture cards of different kinds of weather to my group of students. As I held up one of the cards in front of Suzu, she spoke these words in a whisper - "It is a sunny day." I had to turn away because tears started streaming down my eyes. I couldn't believe that Suzu had finally dared to speak English for the first time. I had to make an on the spot decision as to what reaction would be right for this particularly fragile, ultra shy, non-risk taking student. For, with a different type of student (one who displayed more confidence and was a risk taker), I would have responded with tremendous fanfare in front of the rest of the class. However, based on how delicate Suzu's learning style was, I knew that I'd have to proceed with caution.

In what seemed like a split second, I chose to play this great event down. The children were calling out, "Suzu spoke! She can speak English!" I quietly said, "Isn't it great. Look at that. Suzu has been saving her new words for the right time and now she's ready to use them." Fortunately, from that time on Suzu never stopped talking.

I believe to this day that at that moment there might have been a strong possibility that had I made a big deal of Suzu's first words in front of all her classmates, she would have retreated into herself once again. Instead, I proceeded very gently with lots of love, letting Suzu know on a deep level that she could take risks with me. Additionally, that I was there to not only teach her, but *protect* her as well.

> *"It was the teacher's ability to convey respect and to convey dignity that saved the situation."*
>
> Ginott, 1972

That was the beginning of my long journey of discovery that with all the emphasis on methods courses and curriculum development that I had taken in college, nothing had prepared me for the unique inner complexities of each student who would come before me.

After three years of teaching in a city school, the budget was cut and I lost my job. I got hired to teach E.S.L in a school on Long Island. My knowledge of Portuguese and Spanish was a great asset, since there were many students whose parents were from Portugal and Central and South America.

The students in my E.S.L. classes were grouped according to their English proficiency and grade levels. After spending ten years pulling children out of their regular classrooms for English instruction in my room, I missed having my own self contained class. One of the kindergarten teachers retired, so I decided to make the change from E.S.L. to Kindergarten. I had worked with kindergarten teachers throughout my E.S.L. years, and loved the unbridled enthusiasm of this age group.

Once again, the recurring theme that stood out in my morning and afternoon classes day after day was that there isn't a general formula that will absolutely work when addressing all the needs of each student. What I did know was that in order to maintain a basically happy class, first and foremost I had to establish a caring environment. Then, and only then, would there be an atmosphere where I could see more of a relaxed, authentic representation of the child awaiting my attention.

So, I designed a plan to make a meaningful connection with each student by observing them at storytime, arts and crafts, creative playtime, singing songs, block building, dancing, group lessons, and one on one instructions, etc.

Simple statements like, "I love the way you put these blocks together. Can you tell me something about what you created?" or, "I love the colors that you used in your painting. Would you like to show your painting to the class?" paved the way for what I called an "***intimacy link***" between my students and me.

The four years that I spent in kindergarten were very rewarding. It was such a thrill to see the children blossom, that I thought of how wonderful it would be to move up with them to first grade where they would be using their new readiness skills. I was right.

Teaching first grade has been very gratifying, yet at the same time, extremely challenging. I have had to implement an approach that addresses the academic needs of my students, as well as focuses in on all the information regarding the whole child. This has enabled me to identify the high risk students and address the variables that may be interfering with their academic performance. I've had to try to ascertain the causes for such things as a child's short attention span, distractibility, hyperactivity, depressed appearance, anger outbursts, etc.

All too often these behaviors were directly related or had some connection with a child's home situation. I have witnessed on a regular basis the pain of children who have been traumatized by such scenarios as a death in the family, divorce, both parents working full-time, loss of a job, a move, illness, alcoholism, incarceration of a parent, death of a pet, emotional and/or physical abuse of the spouse or child, not having a parent who speaks English, etc.

"To be protected from destruction, all children, minimally, should live in environments that provide some order and meet their basic physical and material needs. All children should have a continuous relationship with a consistently attentive and caring adult who treat them as special - not as just another inhabitant of this world

- who is able to stimulate appropriate responsibilities and challenges who passes on important social and moral expectations."
Weissbound, 1996

Throughout the pages of my book you will learn how many factors inside and outside the classroom contribute to the success or failure of a child.

This is my personal, heartwarming story of how, by taking on different roles in the classroom (i.e., teacher, parent, nurse, counselor, friend, etc.), I have **NURTURED MY STUDENTS TO SUCCEED!** It has been a journey filled with love, laughter, and sometimes tears.

You are invited to come along and experience the trials and tribulations of our most precious resource - ***OUR CHILDREN***.

Part One

THE IMPORTANCE OF NURTURING OUR CHILDREN IN SCHOOL

"If a man does not keep pace with his companions, perhaps it is because he hears a different drummer. Let him step to the music which he hears, however measured or far away."

HENRY DAVID THOREAU

CHAPTER 1

Starting First Grade As Seen Through The Eyes Of A Six Year Old

Do you remember your beginning days in first grade? If so, take a minute and try to recall what that unique time felt like. For some students the beginning of the first grade school year is a time of much excitement and fun. However, for many students, making the transition from kindergarten to first grade manifests itself as a period filled with lots of anticipatory anxiety.

Year after year, I see their faces in front of me. My students are so vulnerable, so impressionable, often scared, sometimes sad that they had to leave their mothers behind in order to come to school for a full day. There are always those select few who actually have a look of terror in their eyes.

What will school be like for them? Will they like their teacher? Will they make new friends? Will they learn to read? Will they learn to write?

Then, there are the logistical concerns. What will the bus ride by like? How will the bus driver know where to drop them off? Will Mommy be waiting at the bus stop? What happens if she's not? How can they get used to a full day of school? What will they do if school is hard? How will they be able to hold a pencil the correct way? Will they be able to write within the lines? What about trying to hold it in so as not to go to the bathroom often? Who will sit with them in the lunchroom? Where is the lunch room anyway? What if they forget their homework in school? What if they can't do the homework because it's too difficult?

These are just a few of the stresses that students experience at different times during the first days and even weeks of first grade. Yes, there are always those who make a seemingly easy adjustment to the routines. However, even they might be experiencing some hidden discomfort unknown to their parents and/or teacher. As a seasoned educator, *I firmly believe that it is the teacher's responsibility right from the very first days of school to maintain a consistent, meaningful connection with each student by using a manner that is gentle, sensitive, empathic and kind.* Thus, providing the child with the best possible opportunity for feeling relaxed, comfortable and ready to learn.

The tone and volume of a teacher's voice, the expression in a teacher's eyes, as well as her body language can all make the difference in terms of how well her students will relate to her.

Young children are like delicate flowers. In the following exercise I asked my students to draw a picture of how they felt on their first day of first grade. When I asked Alice to tell me about her drawing, she said that she felt like people were going to laugh at her because she's Chinese.

"Children's friendships play a large role in their sense of self, their sensitivity to others and their ability to interact positively with people around them. They compare themselves to their friends, and they learn about their own potential for relating to others in the course of passionate childhood friendships."

Apter, Ph.D., 1997

My first reaction concerning what Alice had disclosed was total surprise accompanied by sadness.

I gently asked Alice if we could talk at my desk area. I had to hold back my tears for I had absolutely no idea based on anything that Alice had

said or done during the school year that she had felt this way.

Alice had been shy at first, but in general she functioned well in all areas of the classroom and had a number of friends.

I could just imagine how difficult the first days of school must have been for her if she could still recall those painful feelings as she drew her picture in June.

When I looked into Alices' eyes I saw so much confidence that I could no longer hold back my tears. Alice had come so far! Her self-esteem had improved quite a bit since September.

With Alice standing by my side I held her hand and said, "Alice do you know that you are a beautiful girl both on the inside and on the outside? I can say that because I've spent all of first grade with you." She stared into my eyes and a big smile appeared on her face as she shook her head and said, "Oh! I know that *now* Ms. Lipper!"

Now, I'd like to share with you what turned out to be one of the most memorable scenarios that I have ever experienced at the start of a school year. It all began with a *Show and Tell*. However, for those of you who aren't familiar with it, let me take the time to describe what it's all about and why I like it so much.

Show and Tell actually begins at home with preparation for the presentation that will be viewed in class. The student, on his own or with help from a parent, selects something from home that he thinks the class will find interesting (i.e., a coin collection, stamp collection, baseball card collection, shell collection, favorite stuffed animal, etc.) and brings it to school. Time permitting, before the actual presentation, I like to have a brief talk with my students so that I can get an idea of what the class will hear. This enables me to screen out any inappropriate discussions. At this age, sometimes a child discloses information that turns out to be too personal to be shared by all. (i.e., one student once said, "I saw my sister kissing her boyfriend in the dark.")

Prior to starting *Show and Tell* I model my own choice item before the class. Last year I brought in some beautiful photos from my hiking trip at Lake Mohonk, New York. I spoke about the history of the area, the magnificent lake, hiking trails, mountains, etc. I tried to be very enthusiastic and engaging. I was able to hold the class captive for those five minutes. It sounds easy, but then I am an adult.

At first, this activity can be very intimidating for a shy child. After one or two times it often works like magic because the student feels so good from meeting success by telling a personal story or describing something special. It's a true thrill to watch this transformation take place. I have derived so much pleasure in witnessing a child's self confidence and pride increase as the year progresses. As depicted in Brian's story, *Show and Tell* helps develop oral communication. It also helps build a child's self-esteem as well as foster healthy peer relations. This challenge also helps to pave the way in preparing a student for such things as reading aloud, participation in a group lesson and story writing.

Now that I've set the *Show and Tell* stage so to speak, you will see why the story that I am about to tell made an everlasting impression upon me.

On *Show and Tell* day, Brian raised his hand and asked if he could speak in front of the class. I called him to my desk and we conferenced about his presentation. Brian said that he'd like to introduce the class to his friend "Waddle" the duck. I said, "Sure, go ahead, but where's Waddle"? Brian was extremely shy. Slowly, he raised his head and looked at me with his big brown eyes. He said, "Ms. Lipper, it's a surprise!" I didn't want to burst his bubble for I was so thrilled that

Brian had the courage to appear in front of the class all by himself, so I said, "Okay, you are next." Brian walked up to the front of the room, but Waddle was nowhere to be seen. I gazed at Brian from my desk, hoping that he wasn't going to lose his confidence. All of a sudden, in a loud voice, Brian said, "I'd like to introduce you to my friend Waddle the duck." This was a real enigma. Well, where was Waddle? What proceeded was one of those moments in teaching that make it all worthwhile.

Catie raised her hand and Brian called on her - "There's no duck there!" She said, with so much certainty in her voice. Brian responded with, "Oh, yes there is! He's sitting on top of Michael's desk. You can't see him because he's invisible." At that point I decided that Brian could use a little support. So, I said, "Brian, tell us a little something about Waddle." With that, Brian said, "Waddle's my imaginary friend. He's been coming to school with me every day." I could see the kids' expressions and wondered what would happen next. Very comfortably, Brian said, "This is his imaginary leash. He stays by my side and waits at the bus stop with me every morning. He sits next to me in the lunchroom. Did you know that Waddle has his own school bag?"

Within a short amount of time all my psychological theories came flooding to the surface. Wow! I thought, Brian is to be commended. What a resourceful way of dealing with his separation anxiety. With the invention of Waddle, Brian had found a way to leave home and confront his fears of attending school.

Instinctively, I knew that this could become a great opportunity to use Brian's creativity as a catalyst for the rest of the class. So, I asked my students to close their eyes and try to imagine spending the rest of the day with an imaginary friend. What would this friend look like? What would you name your friend? What could you and your friend do in school and at home?

Later that afternoon we drew our imaginary friends, made paper bag puppets, and created stories about them. That night I called Brian's mom to find out what kind of feedback he was giving her regarding school. She was very glad that I had called because she was wondering how Brian was doing. She disclosed that he had been having a difficult time leaving for school in the morning. She shared with me the fact that she had given birth to her beautiful daughter in July. Brian wanted to stay home with his little sister. Instead, he had to leave her at home while he attended a full day of school. His mom was pretty sure that Brian was jealous that his sister would have mommy all to herself. Brian's mom was so thrilled to hear that Brian elected to share his imaginary friend with the class. However, she was concerned that Brian would need Waddle for the rest of the school year. I reassured her that when he was ready to, he'd leave Waddle at home. Thankfully, that eventually happened.

This tender tale of Brian and his imaginary friend, Waddle, can serve as a touchstone for all of us. *Every child has his or her own individual needs.* Those needs must be identified, respected and addressed in the best possible way. It is not always necessary for children to conform to guidelines that don't suit them at the time. Can you imagine what would have happened if I had said, "Oh Brian, you are acting so silly. Sit down! There's no such thing as an invisible duck."

> *"But in a recent study of kids between the ages of three and seven, Marjorie Taylor, Ph.D., a professor of psychology at the University of Oregon, confirmed that an imaginary playmate is most likely the result of a healthy social sense and understanding. Taylor's and other studies have found that nearly half of all children have some sort of imaginary companion at some point."*
> Marshall, 1998/99

All of us would have missed out on a great lesson, and much to his detriment, Brian would have been unnecessarily shamed. *WE MUST NURTURE OUR CHILDREN!* **Embrace their creativity!** Teach through love and with love and your students will love to learn.

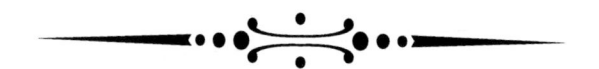

"If you cannot hear the agony and pain of your fellow man, you are no good in this world because it is going to get worse."

Dr. Elisabeth Kubler-Ross

CHAPTER 2

Children in Pain Can't Always Cry

One of my favorite areas in my first grade classroom is what I named the *magic carpet* area. It consists of a small area rug, surrounded by some colorful throw pillows, lots of books, and adorable, huggable stuffed animals that I've collected and the students have named over the years.

At the beginning of the school year, I gather my class together from their formal chairs and desks and introduce them to this space within the room that allows them to travel to far off places through the stories and illustrations of delightful children's literature. We are also blessed to have many stories in big book formats so that all the students can easily see the beautiful illustrations. After I am finished reading the story, they can repeat the text, often learning new words, predicting the endings, making up rhymes, and doing all sorts of reading and phonics skill-related activities.

Before the story begins I ask the children if they would like a stuffed animal to hold in their lap. This further creates a feeling of relaxation so that they can enjoy the story to its fullest.

Other times during the day the children can come to the carpet to work individually or together on extension activities related to the days' lessons.

When I'm not telling a story or teaching a mini lesson, I like to allow students the use of that area as a reward for trying their best, being good listeners, following directions, or just being kind to their classmates.

I usually say something that sounds like this: "Barbara, I love how nicely you are taking care of yourself by following directions and doing your work. Michael, that was so kind of you to lend Robert a pencil. Barbara and Michael, would you like to take your things and go to the *magic carpet* area? You may select your favorite stuffed animal and pillow."

Their faces light up as they proudly gather their necessary books and supplies and continue working on their assignments there. When they are finished, I give them the opportunity to select a story book and read it on the carpet until it's time for the next activity.

This has become an extremely successful technique for teaching responsibility, reinforcing good behavior, and encouraging reading. The children love the *magic carpet* area and take great pride in being chosen to spend productive time there.

Within a few weeks into the school year great things are taking place.

Some of my favorite activities and those of the kids are acting out stories, poetry, story and journal writing, silent reading, reading with a partner, shared group reading, mural making, puzzles, and news of the day.

I'd like to share with you something so touching that happened on that magic carpet. After listening to what took place on that very special day, you will know why I call this chapter "Children In Pain Can't Always Cry."

I had just finished reading a beautiful story to the class. The story was called *Sylvester and the Magic Pebble*, by William Steig. This was a story about a family of donkeys: the mother, father, and Sylvester, the son. Sylvester found a little red pebble while he was walking through a field. He picked it up and soon discovered that this special pebble had magical powers. He learned that whatever he requested came true.

When the story ended, I took out a special pebble, passed it around, and asked the children to hold it in their hands and examine it. Within a few minutes someone said, "Can I make a wish? Can I share it with the class?" So, of course I was thrilled because that was what I had hoped might happen. The magic pebble served as a catalyst for lots of spirited, imaginative conversation. I knew that later on my students would have a terrific opportunity to draw illustrations of their own wishes. Then they would tell and/or write about what they'd wish for and why.

Without warning the lesson quickly took an unpredictable turn. Bobby said that he would love a brand new two-wheeler because he outgrew his tricycle. Karen said that she would wish for a swing set for her backyard so that she could have all her friends over for the afternoon. Sarah said that she wished she could take ballet lessons with her friend Michelle. Sarah loved to dance. However, her mother worked full-time and couldn't fit this added activity into her busy schedule.

Another little boy named Nicholas wished for an electric train set. However, he said that he asked his parents to buy it for him and they didn't have enough money to get it this year. The students were all very quick to give Nicholas suggestions as to how he could save for his wish. The conversation soon became electric.

Shortly thereafter, from the corner of my eye, I glanced at Luis, who had been moving himself closer and closer to the wall. Although Luis' hand wasn't raised, I sensed that Luis wanted to say something to the group. I asked him if he wanted to share his wish, and with that Luis, choking back the tears, said, **"Yes, I wish that I was a baby again so that my mother would hold me in her arms and never let me go."** The other children didn't know why Luis was crying and why he hadn't wished for something new like everyone else. For, you see, Luis was keeping a very painful secret inside. He hadn't been held in his mothers' arms for some time because she was serving out a sentence for committing a drug-related crime. Luis' mother was in jail.

She wasn't working. She wasn't busy with his older brother. She wasn't volunteering her time to help the P.T.A. She was locked behind bars, miles away. Luis and his brother were living with their aunt and uncle. All Luis could ever wish for was to feel the warmth of his mothers' arms wrapped around him and the gaze of her eyes upon his face.

What was I to do? Luckily, it was time for Art. So, I took my class up to the Art room while I asked mi Amor (my educational assistant) to stay on the carpet area with him. (We call her "mi Amor" or "Mrs. Sunshine" because she's full of love and healing, warm energy). She spends about an hour and a half daily in my classroom. I wish that she could be there for at least half the day. As you will see, there is always a student or students who can use her help.

Mi amor sat with Luis on the carpet area until I came back. They enjoyed reviewing the beautiful illustrations of Sylvester and his escapades.

Shortly thereafter, I returned from Art and joined them. Mrs. Sunshine took a walk to the ladies' room so that Luis and I could talk privately. I then asked him if he'd like me to hold him in my arms. He wiped away his tears and said, "Yes, Ms. Lipper, I'd like that." We talked about how much he missed his mom and how we might make her a card because he thought he'd be visiting her soon.

Luis wasn't ready to tell the class that his mother was in jail. However, we talked about how mom would be coming home in a year. Hopefully, she'd be able to hug him forever.

Luis carried a lot of shame around his mother being in prison. He wasn't ready to disclose the details of his situation yet. Therefore, he continued carrying this tremendous weight on his shoulders, trying to keep this secret from his classmates. A few months later, after reading another story, Luis began talking about his life. The children were so loving. They decided to send a large envelope filled with class cards to his mom.

Unfortunately, Luis had a very tough year in first grade. His father left the family when Luis was two years old. His mother was serving a jail sentence. Understandably, Luis felt totally abandoned and different from the other students.

"In the environment of unresolved trauma, mistrust is learned. The child learns, self-contempt rather than self-soothing, fear of aloneness rather than competence, mistrust rather than trust and the development of a reactive self, rather than the development of the unique and beautiful true self."
Middelton-Moz, 1989.

Luis was very athletic and enjoyed playing in the schoolyard with the other kids. However, he found it very difficult to focus on any task for a reasonable period of time. He often arrived late to school, without his homework, or with his homework written in a haphazard, sloppy manner. He would also ask to go to the bathroom frequently. Luis would also get out of his seat and bother other students when I wasn't looking.

Luis, this innocent six-year-old boy, was acting out the intense pain of his family. When his sadness became so unbearable, he'd scream out, "I HATE YOU!" to another child, and "I HATE SCHOOL!!" One day he even screamed, "I HATE THE POLICE! They took away my mommy."

Sadly, I knew about Luis' secret all along. However, in the months prior to reading the Magic Pebble story, I had been advised not to discuss it with him unless he brought it up in class. This had created tremendous frustration and inner turmoil for me.

How could I possibly have looked the other way and have let this child's suffering continue in silence?

Unfortunately, Luis isn't alone. There are children crying out for attention in all the classrooms across our country, although their parents might not be serving time behind bars. Although I found Luis' scenario to be so extreme and out of the ordinary, it happened again years later. Another one of my students suffered from the shame of having a father in prison.

Often, if students and parents do not get the appropriate intervention, the child's behavior may, and often does, interfere with the smooth operation of the class as a whole.

This is similar to the situation where there is a chronically ill child within a family. The parent or parents must focus most of their attention on that child, thus shifting the balance between the other sibling or siblings.

In the following exercise, I asked my students to draw a picture showing what it felt like when something sad happened to them. I asked Sheila to talk about her drawing.

She said that when her parents told her that they were going to get a divorce, she tried to run out of the house. However, her father stopped her before she got to the door. She felt very sad.

"A child of divorcing parents is, like the parents, hurt, angry and confused. There are no means by which a parent, while terminating a partnership, can prevent a child from having these feelings, so feelings should never be ignored, belittled, or denied. We can, however, cushion these feelings and prevent ill effects."
Apter Ph.D., 1997.

24 *Susan Lipper*

In the previous pages you vicariously felt the intensity in which a child's pain was expressed within the walls of my classroom and how it affected all of us as caring human beings. You heard the compelling story of how a simple wish upon a magic pebble turned out to be an enormous cry for help. This, from a little boy who only wanted a hug from his mommy, but couldn't get it because she was in prison.

In the next two pages you will find a guide for the early childhood teacher, as well as a guide for parents. It is my hope that these guides will be helpful in identifying students in crisis.

These are **possible warning signs** to look for associated with a student in need of *intervention*.

A GUIDE FOR THE EARLY CHILDHOOD TEACHER

1. Has difficulty concentrating.

2. Often appears sad and withdrawn.

3. Very rarely participates in daily activities.

4. Rarely shares experiences from home.

5. Changes in appearance (i.e., personal hygiene, cleanliness, clothing) Appears tired.

6. Frequent absences.

7. Frequently arrives late to school.

8. Often forgets lunch money, snack money.

9. Talks about telling changes at home.

10. Demonstrates aggressive behavior.

11. Often calls out (doesn't raise hand to respond).

12. Experiences a great deal of difficulty staying seated.

13. Frequently loses his homework, or didn't do it.

Parents should notify the classroom teacher immediately if they **witness any changes** in their child's usual behavior.

A GUIDE FOR THE PARENTS

1. Often complains of various symptoms upon waking up in the morning (i.e., sore throat, stomach ache, earache, etc.)

2. Often doesn't want to go to school in the morning.

3. Rarely talks about having friends in school.

4. Child almost never shows enthusiasm toward school and its daily activities.

5. Frequently forgets homework assignments in school.

6. Change in regular sleep pattern. Difficulty falling asleep.

7. Repeated nightmares and unusual change in mood.

8. Bedwetting.

9. Unusual behavior at home (i.e., more aggressive, lethargic, etc.)

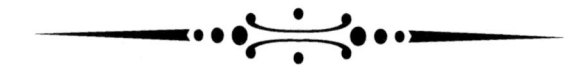

> *"If there's no rain and no nurturing, the seed's going to die."*
>
> — VIRGINIA SATIR

CHAPTER 3

A Look At Some Of My Students

In this chapter you will meet three students, each of whom came to school every day, carrying his or her own personal sadness at such a fragile, young age.

Although each September the names change, the often sad contributing variables that continually distract a child from performing at his or her best remain the same.

How can a child be expected to carry and often try to conceal family pain and still meet success in school?

From my many years of experience in the classroom, I can tell you that it's almost always impossible for a troubled child to work to his full potential.

We as educators must do our best to help our students as they try to cope with circumstances beyond their control.

My students:

George

George was a student in one of my afternoon kindergarten classes. He was the only child of parents who were going through a bitter divorce. George lived in a one bedroom apartment with his mom. She was overwhelmed with her full-time job in a large firm and the responsibility of making sure that her son was being taken care of during the hours that he wasn't at school and she was at work. He had been staying with his grandmother in the mornings.

She would bring George to school and always complained to me about George's behavior. She'd often say something that went like this: "I don't know how you do it Ms. Lipper. George is such a handful. He never listens to me. He's very fresh. He even tells me to shut up and says, "I hate you!" sometimes. Ms. Lipper, I tell my daughter, but it hasn't helped."

In the classroom, George often experienced difficulty interacting with students for a reasonable period of time. He would often have trouble sharing the school materials (i.e., blocks, toys, crayons, etc.) On a few occasions, other children would complain that George was playing rough with them. He did things like grabbing, pushing and throwing items around.

Academically, George experienced lots of difficulty focusing in on the task at hand. In a group lesson he often became distracted. He would frequently get out of his seat and ask to go to the bathroom.

Each afternoon we began our kindergarten class with the calendar, the weather and the news of the day. One day during our news activity George raised his hand. He told the class that his mommy and daddy were always fighting and now they were getting a divorce. He started to cry and said, "Ms. Lipper, it is all my fault that Daddy moved out." I said, "George, it is not your fault. Mommy and Daddy couldn't get along, but they both still love you. They will always be your mommy and daddy." With that he said, "I was a bad boy. I never listened to Mommy or Daddy. I didn't brush my teeth. I didn't clean my room. I didn't eat my breakfast and I made Mommy late for work." With that I held George in my arms, as we both cried.

I explained to George and the class that sometimes mommies and daddies can no longer live together because they can't get along. They try to, but they just can't. So, it's better for them to live apart. It is never, ever the child's fault that their parents decide to get a divorce. All kids do wrong things at one time or another. However, this would never, ever cause mommy or daddy to leave each other. It is between the parents.

> *"You could also talk in some detail about why the marriage did not work. Avoid, as much as possible, attacks on your partner, and focus on the failure of the relationship, rather than on the faults of either person. Such explanations will fill in the background to the break-up, and make it more difficult for the child to conclude that it must be her fault."*
>
> Apter, Ph.D., 1997.

Unfortunately, what George was feeling is all too common. Very often, younger children blame themselves for their parents' divorce. **THEY THINK IT WAS SOMETHING THAT THEY DID OR DIDN'T DO.**

That night I called George's mom and explained what had happened during the news of the day! She had no idea that George was blaming himself. Eventually, George and his mom went for family counseling outside of the school so that George could work it through and express his feelings.

By the end of the school year, George seemed much more relaxed, focused, and ready to learn.

Cindy

Cindy was one of my first students in my E.S.L. class at my school on Long Island where I have taught for the last twenty years. This school is in a middle-class community, comprised of children from many ethnic backgrounds. There are a fair number of homes in which English is the second language—Portugese, Spanish, Chinese, Japanese, Greek, Italian, etc. are spoken between parents and children. The majority of the E.S.L. students speak either Portugese or Spanish.

Cindy was a very shy first grader, who always kept to herself. Her parents were born in Portugal. They came to the United States to make a better life for themselves.

Cindy's language skills were improving. However, she always seemed sad, withdrawn and very rarely spoke to the other students in the group.

We had been working on our "All About Me" books. In this book, the students drew pictures of their families, friends, school and wrote stories about all their favorite hobbies and interests, etc.

One day I asked the children to draw their self portraits. I modeled the lesson by demonstrating a drawing of myself. I pointed out my hair and eye color, clothing, hair length, height, jewelry, etc. I explained to the students that they should do the best that they could. I wasn't going to judge their drawings. Whatever they drew would be fine.

I asked everyone if they understood what to do, and said that anyone needing help should come up to me. Well, everyone got started promptly. However, Cindy sat there with this terribly sad look on her face. I walked over to her desk and whispered to her privately, "Do you need some assistance?" She said, "No," and began to cry. I asked her to take her paper and crayon and come to my desk.

Once we got to my desk, I asked Cindy what was wrong. She said that she didn't want to draw a picture of herself because she was ugly. I looked into her eyes and told her that she was so beautiful. With that, she said, "No I'm not, Ms. Lipper. I hate my face. Don't you see! I have to wear these big ugly glasses. The kids make fun of me. I hate them."

Sure enough, I could see why Cindy was feeling so bad about her glasses and why she felt they made her look ugly. They were old fashioned, large, dark, and an unflattering style. They detracted from her appearance and hid her sparkling eyes. I quickly took out my hand mirror and asked Cindy to look at herself in it. I looked at her at the same time. With my arm around her shoulder, I said, "Cindy, I see a beautiful, kind, and smart young lady. I bet you'd like a different pair of glasses; a pair that would be colorful and make you feel beautiful." Sure enough, she said, "I would, Ms. Lipper."

So, with that, I told Cindy that I'd speak to her mother. Cindy started to cry again. She said, "My mother and father don't have any money." She wasn't wrong. Her parents were both working for minimal wages at the factory. They had an older daughter and three younger sons to support. I said, "Leave it to me, Cindy. Let me see what I can do." Cindy expressed that she was afraid that her parents would be angry at her for not liking her glasses. I said that I promised I'd speak to her mom and she wouldn't get in trouble.

That night I called the P.T.A. president, and the P.T.A. Assistance Fund eventually was able to help Cindy's mom get Cindy a more modern, attractive pair of glasses.

Cindy drew a beautiful self portrait that reflected her true inner spirit. She began to speak in a louder voice, and held her head up for all to see. When I spoke to her mom on Open School Night, she thanked me so much and said that Cindy's new glasses made Cindy so happy.

How a child sees herself can make all the difference in her ability to meet success in school. A new pair of eyeglasses allowed Cindy to actually see herself in all her true beauty for the first time in a long time.

Dorothy

Dorothy was a student in one of my first grade classes. She was one of three children. She had two older brothers. One was in the middle school, and one was in the fourth grade.

Dorothy always came to school wearing a big smile on her face. It seemed as though she couldn't wait to start the day. She loved her fellow classmates, and was always very complimentary and demonstrative towards me. She would say things like, "Ms. Lipper, you look so pretty today", or, "Ms. Lipper, I love your bracelet." Often, after I finished reading a story to the class on the *magic carpet*, Dorothy would run up to me, put her arms around my neck, kiss me on the cheek, and say, "Ms. Lipper, I love you!"

Watching that scene, no one would ever have known what a sad home life Dorothy had, and how her background had contributed to so many learning problems in school.

Unfortunately, Dorothy was born with Fetal Alcohol Syndrome. During her pregnancy,

Dorothy's mom drank all kinds of alcoholic beverages. Dorothy was born prematurely and weighed very little at birth. Her first years were very difficult. She was language delayed. She didn't speak until she was three and a half years old, she didn't walk until she was two and a half years old, and she had difficulty with her gross motor skills like climbing, running, catching and throwing a ball, etc.

A year ago, Dorothy's father was arrested on theft charges and was serving out a three year sentence in prison. She missed him a lot and talked about him all the time. Dorothy lived in her grandma's house with her mom and two brothers. Her mom suffered from a herniated disk in her back. Therefore, she was home most of the time, receiving disability. The one person Dorothy always spoke about was her grandma. For it was her grandma who always read to her, helped her with her homework, and physically cared for her.

Dorothy experienced a great deal of difficulty processing one, two and three step directions in school. She also had difficulty pronouncing many words and forming whole sentences. Since kindergarten, she had been getting occupational therapy to help her with her writing and cutting.

She also received speech therapy to improve her language development and pronunciation skills.

As a result of her mom's condition during pregnancy, Dorothy had a hard time remembering numbers and the names of the letters of the alphabet and their sounds.

As often as possible, she would receive one on one guidance and instruction from our educational assistant. However, in a group, Dorothy often became lethargic and easily distracted.

Three things that Dorothy loved were singing, dancing and drawing pictures. Through those three areas, Dorothy gained a lot of confidence.

I will never forget the morning when Dorothy fell asleep at her desk. The student sitting next to her came up to me while I was working with a reading group and said, "Ms. Lipper, Dorothy is sleeping." This was unusual for Dorothy, so I went to see this for myself. I tapped Dorothy lightly on the shoulder and whispered her name so as not to startle her. I asked her if she was okay. She said, "Ms. Lipper, I don't feel well." With that, I felt her forehead and realized that she probably had a fever.

I sent her to the nurse. The nurse called her mother and asked her to take Dorothy home.

When Dorothy's mother got to school she told the nurse that she knew that Dorothy wasn't feeling well that morning. She had begged Dorothy to stay home, but Dorothy cried and said that she loved school and didn't want to miss anything.

For Dorothy, school was the primary stabilizing force in her life. She felt special, she received lots of attention, was made to feel successful, and was working at her own pace.

By the end of the school year Dorothy was beginning to function on a first grade level. She could recognize sight words, read simple sentences, and write simple stories using inventive spelling.

Unfortunately, in July Dorothy's grandma died of a heart attack. That August the family moved out of state to be closer to Dorothy's aunt and cousins. I think about Dorothy all the time, and pray that she is doing well.

"Only those who dare to fail greatly can achieve greatly"

ROBERT F. KENNEDY

CHAPTER 4

Creating a Learning Environment That is Safe For Children to Take Risks

The great news is that it can be done and must be done. The early childhood grades are the foundation for all the years to come. A learning environment that is safe for children to take risks is an environment where children will feel good about themselves and will grow academically as well.

The kind of creativity that flows from a risk-taking, safe learning environment can be extraordinary. I know because I have seen it. The classroom teacher needs to be extremely sensitive to the developmental difficulties among her students. *The teacher's goal must be to maximize a child's self-esteem by helping him meet success at his own particular level.*

Children have different learning styles and are differently influenced by the various stimuli in the classroom environment.

Throughout my years of teaching, I have developed different techniques to motivate my students to take risks without them feeling ashamed if they don't succeed on the first try. Posted throughout the room I have different sayings that my children can refer to and gain confidence and direction from. Inside a big gold star is written *"You Are A Shining Star!"* Each one of us is special in our own way. Each one of us shines within the classroom universe making it a vast, spectacular place for discovery.

Every morning I hold up a sign that says please remember to LOOK! LISTEN! And LEARN! (It has a pair of eyes, ears, and a book next to the words as a visual reminder.) I explain to my class that if they pay attention and look my way, listen carefully to what I and the other students have to say, they will learn something new every day.

One of my favorite sayings is **"If at first you don't succeed, try, try again!"** (I added) **"Even teachers make mistakes!"** "BE GOOD TO YOURSELF!"

To demonstrate what I mean by this saying, throughout the school year I disclose to my students stories from my own childhood that illustrate times when I attempted to do something, began to think that I couldn't, almost gave up, but ultimately kept trying until I tried my best

Nuturing Our Children To Succeed **43**

Friendly Reminders

"If at first you don't succeed try, try again!"

"Even teachers make mistakes!"

"Be good to yourself!"

By: Angie

Please Remember to

⭐ 1 Look

⭐ 2 Listen

⭐ 3 Learn

Brown Bear

or succeeded at what I was trying to do. I always reenact that time of my childhood when I was their age. Like the time that I learned to ride a two-wheeler bicycle for the first time. I fell so many times, but kept on trying, and eventually succeeded. I tell the story with tremendous enthusiasm, as if I were one of them. Halfway into the reenactment I can see that every face is fixated on me, and they are wondering what will happen next. Not only have they learned a lesson that can help them to tackle difficult tasks, moreover they have seen me, and felt my open, loving heart. They know by example that I was once one of them. If I went through it and succeeded, so can they, which has just paved the way for risk-taking. Here is where we form that *intimacy link* that I spoke about in my introduction. I explain to them that even now as an adult, as a teacher, I make mistakes.

> *"Teachers who want to improve relations with children, need to unlearn their habitual language of rejection and acquire a new language of acceptance. To reach a child's mind a teacher must capture his heart. Only if a child feels right can he think right."*
>
> Ginott, 1972.

As the year progresses, they love pointing out a mistake on the blackboard that I've written.

They will always say, "That's okay Ms. Lipper, even teachers make mistakes!"

Another technique that I use to motivate my students to take risks without feeling ashamed if they don't succeed on the first try is called *the magic screen.*

I developed this tool because I found that often, even if a child tried to form a letter on an unlined paper, if the letter was written incorrectly the student would become frustrated, and sometimes give up after seeing that his letter didn't look like the perfectly formed sample.

With this tool, the students form their letters by first using their pointer finger on their desk top. I call their desk top *the magic screen.*

I walk around the room standing behind them, watching as they practice forming the letters on their *magic screen.* I'll emphasize forming the letter from top to bottom, down and around, etc. When they are ready, from there they go on to pencil and paper, and usually have an easier time forming the letters correctly.

Sometimes, as adults we tend to forget the difficulties that children experience when they attempt to do a task for the first time. Aside from the logistics of forming the letters, a child can be made to feel inadequate if he is criticized for not having a perfect finished product. I recall hearing the phrase like a mantra in my education courses. *"It's not the product that's important. It's the process!"* Well, this is one of the most important things to remember in teaching younger children.

A perfectly formed *A* is not going to be a deciding factor in a child's life. However, the way in which a student is instructed and guided, and whether or not she is ultimately encouraged and praised for trying her best at forming the letter A will contribute toward setting the stage toward future risk-taking.

To get a firsthand feeling for what I am saying, take a piece of lined paper and a pen. Use your non-dominant hand (the hand that you don't usually write with) and try to form a perfect upper and lower case *B b*, making sure that you start from top to bottom. Try to focus on staying within the lines. How does this make you feel? You can certainly empathize with the frustrations that a child may have to endure when writing, cutting, or even coloring within the lines.

I have just shared with you but a few of the techniques that I use within my classroom so that a child can feel relaxed and open toward the whole learning process.

For the following assignment, I asked two of my former students to draw a picture of something that they did, that originally they didn't think they could do. I asked them to specifically choose a task that they felt good about.

In this first drawing, you can see Kimberly sitting at her computer. You will notice that her dad is saying, "Good." I am sure that the praise that her father gave Kimberly helped her to gain confidence in this new area. Kimberly told me that at first she didn't think she could remember what to do. Now she feels that using computers is so much fun. She said, "Ms. Lipper, if I can do it, anyone can do it!"

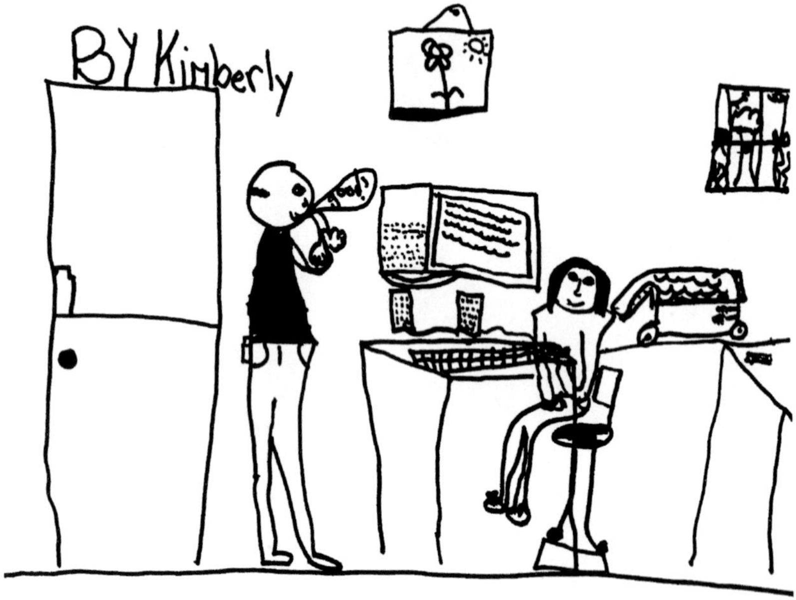
BY Kimberly

In this drawing, Melissa shows herself ice-skating. She explained to me that this was when she went ice-skating with her Brownie Troop. She thought that she wouldn't be able to skate, but she did. Melissa said, "Ms. Lipper, I thought I couldn't do it. I thought I couldn't skate! But I could you see, because I *kept trying!*"

I was about to end this chapter with Melissa's drawing, when I could hear a child's voice within me say, "but Ms. Lipper, what about when you make us laugh!"

It is not so easy for me to share this with you because it's something that came naturally for me since the first day I stepped into a classroom. I have used it many times, every day when appropriate, throughout the course of my over twenty years of teaching. It is levity, humor, comedy, laughter, and fun. I am asking myself this question right now. How do you teach other teachers how to be funny in the classroom? Truthfully, I don't know. I can only tell you that it has made for the best times in my career. *Children need to laugh*!

As Victor Borge so beautifully put it: **"Laughter is the shortest distance between two people."**

BY Melissa

Think about it. Adults need to laugh, too. You know how you feel after a good laugh. It's some sort of release from your every day tensions and worries (if just for that minute). You feel refreshed and somewhat relaxed. Your mood often improves.

Well, laughter and children go hand-in-hand. I have been able to make the most serious, shy, tense, scared children laugh. Once I have disarmed them, a great metamorphosis occurs. My students respond with a big smile. We become connected through love, laughter and fun. My lessons expand and are more creative as my classroom becomes charged with enthusiasm.

I can give you a few examples of some funny things that I incorporate into my morning routine. Every morning I have to find out what the children are ordering from the lunchroom. That is called the lunch count. After a while, it can become frustrating because six and seven year old children often change their request at the last minute (i.e., they order a hamburger, and when I'm ready to send the slip in they decide they want a bagel). So, I might say, "Okay. How many of you want bubble gum sandwiches for lunch?" It's so silly, but with the timing and their age, they laugh and laugh. Or, right away a child will ask, "Ms. Lipper, can I go to the bathroom?" I'll say yes. As they're leaving, I'll say, "You must give me one hundred dollars." They'll look worried, and I'll say, "Okay. I'll take fifty dollars." We get down to twenty-five cents, and they say, "Ms. Lipper, that's my snack money." With that, I'll say, "I'm only kidding", and they laugh. After a while, I have had some of my really shy children wait for me to do this routine, just because they enjoy the banter.

Every day we go over the weather. So, once in a while I'll say, "Look out the window! It's cloudy with a chance of meatballs!" (This came from a book by the same title). They laugh!

When we are ready to get on line to go to Art, Music, Gym, etc., sometimes I'll say, "Stand up, push your chairs in, and put on your pajamas!" Instead of, "stand up, push your chairs in and get on line." Of course, they laugh.

In the beginning of the year I have to check to make sure that the bus children go on the correct bus lines, and that the walkers go on their lines. Once in a while I'll say, "Who came to school by helicopter? Get on the helicopter line."

I am sure that by now you have had enough of my elementary school humor. Truthfully, the kids love it. They love to laugh. Unfortunately, many of us don't laugh enough. Again, this comfort level contributes to the risk-taking atmosphere in the classroom because my students know that I will be kind to them.

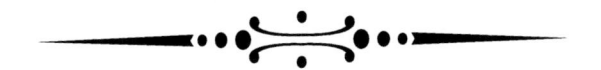

"Character building begins in our infancy, and continues until death."

ELEANOR ROOSEVELT

CHAPTER 5

The Importance of Character Building

To foster self-respect, self-esteem and respect for others, character building is a theme that every student benefits from. Over and over again, children come away from my class feeling proud that they know the importance of doing something kind, helping others. The ultimate reward is that by helping others they feel good about themselves.

There's a video on this topic, available at most libraries, that I like to show my students. It's an episode of Mister Roger's neighborhood called *Kindness*. It runs approximately one half hour long. The tape emphasizes how when you are not nice, or when you are not being kind to someone else, you'll make the other person feel bad and sad. It further points to the lesson that it's not important what a person is like on the outside. What's important is how kind that person is on the inside. Through Mister Roger's kind manner, he reinforces the idea that being kind to others will help us feel good about ourselves.

At the beginning of every school year we recite a variation of *The Golden Rule*. It goes like this - **"Please treat others the way you would want them to treat you! - with kindness, with patience, and with love."** On a regular basis we repeat this motto as needed.

This is how I designed my class poster:

The reason I added with kindness, with patience and with love is because many young children need to mentally visualize things through modeling and examples. This way, when it comes to making a choice as to how to behave in a situation, hopefully they will have a point of reference so that they can do the right thing.

When a classmate is trying to decode a new word out loud during a group lesson, or another student is trying to stay within the lines on the blackboard, the other children learn to be patient, and with positive reinforcement they even volunteer to be of help.

The students become accustomed to my style of speaking to them. I try my best to verbally acknowledge a situation within the day where a child did something kind for a fellow classmate.

"PLEASE TREAT OTHERS THE WAY YOU WANT THEM TO TREAT YOU."
"WITH KINDNESS
WITH PATIENCE
WITH LOVE!!"
By: Angie

I will say something like, "Carlos, I like the way you shared your snack with Michael. His mom didn't have time to pack a snack this morning because she was running late for work. You really helped out. That made him feel good. Thank you. That was an act of kindness."

There have been times when the whole class was working on an assignment and a child raised his hand and said, "Ms. Lipper, can I talk to you?" I said, "Sure, come over to my desk." He stood by my side and said, "Ms. Lipper, Roberta is crying because she can't find her pencil and she forgot what to do." I thanked the student, called Roberta, solved the crisis, and acknowledged the act of kindness that took place. This type of classroom talk creates a very positive tone. It decreases the occasions that students say and do inappropriate things to each other.

"Whenever possible, reward good behavior rather than punish poor behavior. Rewarding a child's positive behavior is far more conducive to self-esteem than is punishment of poor behavior."
                                   Apter, Ph.D., 1997

For the following exercise, I asked my students to draw a picture of something that they did that was kind to someone else. In this drawing Jose drew a picture of himself helping his mom bake

By Jose

cookies. That's an act of kindness practiced at home.

A few years ago I took the theme of kindness and designed a school-wide program which encouraged students throughout the grades to practice *Acts of Kindness*. I wrote a simple kindness song that the students sang with pride. It went like this! (To the tune of the Eency Weency Spider):

Practice Acts of Kindness

Practice acts of kindness
each and every day.

Practice acts of kindness
you can lead the way.

The world will be a better place
for every one of us.

So practice acts of kindness
Each and every day!

With the first assembly that I put together to raise the consciousness of our students grade K-5, I introduced songs, poems and told a story depicting kind acts using my puppets. Later on that year, I dedicated an *Acts of Kindness* flag to our school, with the symbol of two red hearts on it. This flag flew beside the American flag on the front lawn of our school to remind everyone to be kind to each other.

I also *introduced* an *Acts of Kindness* campaign. Students wrote on a piece of paper or told their teacher about some act of kindness that they had witnessed at school. Teachers participated as well. On Friday mornings, the *acts of kindness* were announced over the intercom for the whole school to share. It truly became *cool* to help a student in school.

We sponsored a bumper sticker contest. The winning sticker showed two hands grasping a heart and the slogan said, *"Practice Acts of Kindness! We Do!"*

Proof that the *Acts of Kindness* campaign met with success was when one of the kindergartners saw me in the hall and shouted out, "I know you! You are the *acts of kindness* lady!" That was a title that I wore so proudly.

Later on in the school year, I created a radio D.J. called *Radio Rhonda*. Every Friday on the intercom I shared poems and stories written by the students on topics related to our kindness theme. My call letters were WAOK - where it was okay to practice *Acts Of Kindness*.

I have witnessed remarkable transformations in the way in which children relate to each other. Practice acts of kindness! You can lead the way for our children!

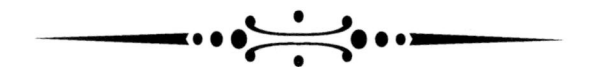

"Nobody sees a flower - really - it is so small it takes time - we haven't time - and to see takes time, like to have a friend takes time."

GEORGE O'KEEFE

CHAPTER 6

The Need For Smaller Classes With Educational Assistants

The good news is that the need for smaller class size, especially in grades K-2, is finally being recognized from the president down to the governors of many states within our country. That is because research indicates that reduced class size in the early childhood grades significantly contributes to improvement in long term student achievement for the two most important curriculum areas - Reading and Math. (Fifteen to seventeen students is optimum in class size).

When a teacher has twenty-two to twenty-five students in a class without help from an educational assistant, she is really spreading herself thin. The younger the child, the more arduous it is for her to follow two and three step directions. This difficulty is exacerbated when the instructions are given in front of a large group of children.

Try saying to a first grade class, "Take your handwriting books out. Put them on your desks. Now, turn to page six." Some children will just be so overwhelmed with hearing any direction that they'll call out, "What did you say?" "I don't know what to do." "I can't remember what you said!" Others will take out the wrong books. Still, others will ask, "What book?" Just glance at what's happening around the room. You'll even see and hear a few students ask their classmates what page to turn to.

In my first grade classes the chronological age of my students was usually six or seven. However, within that limited age range, there were always children performing on reading and math levels starting as low as Pre-K, while extending to as high as third grade.

To complicate matters, there were always diversified developmental and emotional needs within my classes. For example, during the first few months of school, one child might require four minutes to write her name, while another required less than a minute. A new first grader might ask to go to the bathroom two or three times in one hour (due to separation anxiety, performance anxiety, etc.), while his classmate might not have to go until lunchtime.

For these inexperienced students, just getting prepared to work can and often becomes a *Herculean* task.

Based on my own experiences, and after speaking with many of my colleagues over the years, there seems to be a unanimous feeling among educators, and parents as well, that small group instruction is much more advantageous to the class as a whole and the individual child.

From my interactions over the years, I can attest to the fact that when I had a smaller class (anywhere from eighteen to twenty-one students), I was able to scan the room more easily to see if there were students who were in need of help.

I have been blessed throughout my career with having a teacher's aide in each one of my classrooms. From the time I met my first right-hand woman (they have always been women), I was elated that there would be another pair of eyes, ears and hands to work by my side to help me with the demands necessitated by my daily routine. My school district uses the term teacher aides. However, from the inception, I have called these special people *educational assistants* because they have truly assisted me in all aspects of the educational components that make for a productive, happy classroom.

My only complaint is the limited time in which they worked in my room each day. It ranged anywhere from one hour to about an hour and fifteen minutes. (Each first grade teacher received an equal amount of assistance).

It is my firm belief that there should be an educational assistant for at least half a day (full day would be preferable) in every first grade classroom throughout the country. I have had first-hand experience with the many ways in which she can help to make learning easier and more productive for the individual child.

As I continually identified the needs of my students, I was able to prescribe specific programs of instructions which my educational assistant then implemented. First and foremost, I had her observe the techniques I used with a particular student. Then, I would observe her interaction as she worked with the child. Sometimes, I'd make suggestions, depending on what transpired. (For example, if she was helping a child write his name and I noticed that he needed more time practicing each letter before he wrote his full name, I'd explain and model this for her).

My educational assistants have been successful in reaching children in need of additional assistance or remediation. On the other end of the learning curve, they have devoted time to those students who were functioning on or above grade level. This helped them to remain motivated, engaged in, and challenged by their daily assignments. *Every child needs some individual attention.* There have been many times when my educational assistants have helped in addressing the needs of children in crisis. Their kind, gentle manner instantly soothed and nurtured the student at hand.

I don't know what I would have done without these giving jewels.

> *"Some aides also tutor students individually and in small groups. They save the teacher time and energy and create favorable conditions for teaching and learning."*
> Ginott, 1972.

> "The problem is never the problem; it's the coping with the problem that makes the problem."
>
> — Virginia Satir

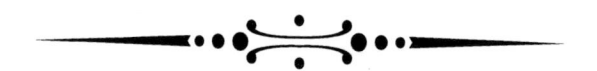

CHAPTER 7

A Multi-Level Approach To Helping Our Students

As each school year unfolds, by working closely with my students, I become aware of the various academic and/or emotional concerns regarding the way in which they are functioning in my classroom.

Ultimately, I use my judgment, based on my professional expertise, to determine whether or not my concerns warrant further scrutiny by our school team. This team (often called the child study team), consists of all or most of these professionals: the principal, school psychologist, speech therapist, nurse, learning specialist and resource room teacher.

Here is a profile of one of my students who needed intervention. Peter loved doing *Show and Tell*. He had a terrific love for nature, science and computers. Each Friday, he would raise his hand and make a fabulous *Show and Tell* presentation, often using sophisticated vocabulary words. My other first graders would marvel at his level of confidence.

However, when it came to recognizing numbers, letters of the alphabet, and sounds, Peter consistently became very frustrated. He often liked to day dream or play with the school supplies in his desk. After having a conference with his mom, I found out that Peter was having difficulty completing any homework assignment related to his reading and math work.

To eliminate the possibility that he needed glasses, his mom took him to an ophthalmologist. It turned out that he did need glasses.

Even with his glasses, I continued to notice that Peter was experiencing difficulty and was becoming more and more frustrated with his daily lessons. I was very concerned that this would negatively affect Peter's self-esteem. Moreover, I was afraid that he might lose his wonderful enthusiasm for learning. So, I brought Peter's case before the child study team.

The child study team listened to my concerns and agreed that I should write out a referral for Peter. The referral explains a student's classroom strengths and needs along with any additional background information that will help paint an accurate picture of the child as a whole. Then, with his parents' permission, we would begin the process of finding out what was interfering with his learning, and then make a recommendation. This took a few weeks.

After all of the specialists involved did their testing, I brought his work samples to help illustrate my concerns (notebook work, math work, handwriting practice, drawings, inventive spelling, etc.) We all got together in the principal's office to review the results. It turned out that Peter had a learning disability called dyslexia.

Peter's parents were very relieved to find out that Peter would be receiving Resource Room services a few times a week for the rest of the school year. I was thrilled that Peter was going to receive the help that he needed.

Peter loved going to his Resource Room class, where he worked with a group of three other children. The Resource Room teacher shared her techniques with me to assist Peter in his reading, math and writing activities. Shortly thereafter, she met with Peter's mom to familiarize her with techniques that she could use at home.

Within a few weeks, I witnessed so many positive changes in Peter, both academically and emotionally.

Peter's story had a very happy ending. However, there have been times when I have felt frustrated with the general process of finding the best remedy for a child in crisis. By that I mean addressing the needs of a child who is acting out his or her emotional pain in the classroom on an almost regular basis.

There must be a stronger emphasis on feedback from the classroom teacher. The classroom teacher's observations are the most consistent and the most accurate. She is able to take notice of a child's behavior at the start of the school day, before snack, after lunch, in the halls, on the class line, at his desk, in the reading group, in the clothing closet, etc. On a daily basis, she can see whether he takes risks, seems frightened, has friends, is withdrawn, etc. *A strong emphasis on feedback* from the classroom teacher can make all the difference in properly assessing and prescribing a program that will best meet the child's needs and will benefit the rest of his classmates as well.

"Tests are of little value and may even be harmful when they are used only to label and sort students. Assessment results should be considered as one piece of a puzzle, not "the answer" to the problem." In planning instructional programs, teachers, counselors,

school psychologists, parents, and students should look at all the evidence they have."
Olivier and Bowles, 1996.

Over the last ten years I have seen the number of children of divorced parents double. Too often these children have a host of issues that may, and often do, interfere with their daily performance.

We need full-time social workers in our schools throughout our country to run ongoing programs to help children process their feelings when necessary.

I observed a program called the *Banana Splits*, run by a wonderful mental health professional in another school district on Long Island. The children of divorce met on a weekly basis in a forum guided by love and professional support. They had a place where they could release their pain and share their sadness with children who were in a similar situation. The social worker used art activities, puppets, music, role playing, etc. She said, "Ms. Lipper, the children no longer feel alone!!"

I do firmly believe (and everyone who knows me knows that I am passionate about this) that there should be one full-time mental health professional on staff in every elementary school nationwide. Whether they are social workers or psychologists it doesn't necessarily matter, as long as they are available on a regular basis to meet with children in need of support. Moreover, it is mandatory that every child in crisis be seen by this professional to receive the proper intervention.

The mental health professional must approach the child with love and through love. He must be first and foremost a good communicator with the rest of the staff. His role can be of the greatest value to the classroom teacher.

The classroom teacher needs to be able to come to a social worker or school psychologist for suggestions. She needs to feel that she is helping her students in need of emotional support.

The mental health professional can and should do workshops for parents and teachers on an array of topics such as working and relating to children of divorce, the hyperactive child, the angry child, the depressed child, etc.

We have all seen the violence in the middle and high schools on television. (Teenagers shooting other teenagers.) I am so sorry to say that I wasn't shocked by that intense level of rage because I have witnessed it in the early grades in a different form. Where will our angry six and seven year old children be ten years from now? We must address the whole child, not just his or her academic statistics.

Our children are in need of help, and our parents are in need of help as well. Often, one or both of the divorced parents remarries, which often creates a host of other problems (i.e., stepfather, stepmother, stepsister, stepbrother). The issue of the single parent family is even more taxing for the child and the parent, especially when that parent is working full-time (i.e., finances, baby-sitting, housework, etc.)

As teachers, we need to know that our principals will be *proactive* when it comes to addressing not only the academic, but the social and emotional needs of a child as well. A teacher's request for intervention must be heard, or the classroom situation will eventually worsen.

A principal cannot hesitate to intervene when a child's behavior is regularly interfering with the healthy operation of the rest of the class.

Our principals must consistently establish and maintain open and honest communication with their teachers. It is paramount that they encourage and honor the teacher's feedback, trust the teacher's judgment, and ultimately take action to ensure the emotional and physical well being of the child in question, as well as the stability of the rest of the class.

As the father (magnificently portrayed by the late Marcello Mastroianni) sadly found out in the movie *Stanno Tutti Bene* (Italian for Everybody's Fine), everybody was not always fine. The lives of his adult children were plagued with all sorts of problems. Unfortunately, they were just too afraid to speak their truth to him. So, whenever he asked, "How's everybody doing?", they responded with "Everybody's fine!"

If a principal really wants to help his students, he must be willing to hear the truth from his teachers and act on it. Or, when he asks a teacher, "How's everybody doing?", she might just respond with, *"Everybody's fine!"*

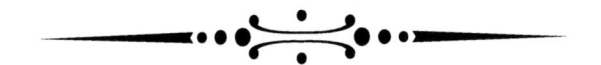

"The world is all gates, all opportunities, strings of tension awaiting to be struck."

RALPH WALDO EMERSON

CHAPTER 8

Establishing Healthy, Productive Communication Between Parent and Teacher

I always look forward to *Meet Your Teacher Night,* for that is the time when I set the ground work for establishing healthy, productive communication with the parents of the children in my class.

It all begins on that very special evening. Prior to the talk, parents receive a note from school explaining that their attendance is very important. A few days beforehand, I ask my students to draw a picture to leave on their desks for their parents to see. They can write "*I LOVE YOU*" on it or "*WELCOME TO SCHOOL*", something short and sweet for their parents to take home.

I also discuss the importance of this night with my students so they can *encourage their parents* to come to school. *Studies show that when a parent is involved in a child's school, the student's self-esteem and academic growth improve.* It gives a child a tremendous sense of pride to know that her parent deeply cares about what is going on and how she is doing in class. The underlying message that children can get if their parent or parents are not involved is that they don't matter enough for their parents to take the time to get involved. By not being proactive in a child's education, a parent can be sabotaging his child from reaching his full potential without really knowing it. That is why I make every effort to encourage a good turnout.

It is at *Meet Your Teacher Night* where I speak from my heart and explain my classroom philosophy. Hopefully, when the parents leave that evening they will feel confident in knowing that the year ahead will be fun, creative and very productive.

Here's how the meeting begins. First, I ask the parents to sit at their child's desk. (Name tags are displayed). This gives me an opportunity to glance around the room and connect the child with the parent. Then, I introduce myself, and explain how first and foremost I pride myself in consistently maintaining open communication with all of them throughout the school year.

Just as my primary goal has always been to establish an *intimacy link* with my students, this goal holds true for the parents of my students as well. **By establishing this intimacy link with**

the parents, we can become partners in meeting the needs of the child. In order for me to address the concerns of the whole child and how any variable in her life might be effecting her well-being in school, I explain to the parents that I need their feedback whenever there is a situation that might warrant my knowledge and possible involvement.

Accordingly, we as a team can work together in addressing the variables that might affect their child's happiness and ability to focus and perform in school. For example, I ask, "Has there been any recent changes at home?" (i.e., marital separation, divorce, illness, move, death in the family, loss of job, etc.).

Regarding school, I explain that they should let me know if their child seems to be upset or concerned about any area of school (i.e., difficulty doing the homework, child feels sad because she doesn't have any friends or children are being mean).

I let the parents know that they can call me at school. I will get a message in my box. Depending upon the situation, I will return their call when the children are dismissed or from my home later on that night. If the concern is not urgent, they can write me a letter. I'll be sure to respond with a note or phone call as soon as possible.

I look forward to a parent's feedback, for a parent knows his child more intimately than anyone else. I tell the parents that any information that is disclosed to me is held in the strictest confidence.

If a parent has a concern about his or her child prior to the first conference date, I encourage them to make an appointment to see me. Likewise, I explain to the parents that I will be sure to contact them if I feel there is such a need.

At this meeting I also inform them that we will be scheduling a conference time to talk about their child's progress in school. It is imperative that each parent attend. The school has set up day and evening conferences to accommodate different schedules.

I let the parent know that I will want their children to come to this session with them. This way I can speak to the parent first and then have the child join us. This allows me to share my information concerning the student's progress with the parent privately. Then I explain to the parent that I will model the methods I use in the classroom with their child.

The parent gets an opportunity to see what their child is doing, and he also learns ways in which to work with her. I have had terrific conferences based on this technique. I also make sure to model and emphasize the way I encourage and praise the child without ever shaming him for not getting the correct answer.

Ultimately, I use this conference as an excellent opportunity for strengthening that *intimacy link* between teacher and student, teacher and parent, parent and student, and finally, most importantly, teacher, parent and student as a joint team.

I try my best to make every parent feel relaxed. They are often living vicariously through their child, as well as remembering their own early school years and how difficult it might have been. Therefore, it is not so unusual for them to feel concerned and sometimes overwhelmed with an issue affecting their child.

I always try to present the child's strengths, as well as the child's needs, in a very, very sensitive manner. I want the parent to know that I am on their child's side. Secondly, I want the parent to know that I will always try my best to work with them to help their child meet success in school.

One example of parent/teacher communication working at its best took place when I taught kindergarten. At my first conference with Carl's mom, she was able to share her fears for her child.

She explained to me how her son was very, very shy. It troubled her to see him this way because she could recall all too well the painful experiences of her own childhood as an extremely shy little girl. I greatly appreciated her candor, and could see in her eyes and feel from the tone in her voice how difficult it was for her to talk about this personal issue. I thanked her and let her know how much she had helped her child by sharing this background information with me.

With my heightened sensitivity to Carl's social and emotional development and learning style, throughout the course of the year I was able to help him overcome his shyness and excel in all areas of the school setting.

At the end of kindergarten, I received a beautiful note from Carl's mom expressing her gratitude for making Carl's first school experience such a good one.

Carl's mom became a true advocate for her son. She made *all* the difference in the world!

The last paragraph of the following poem entitled *Two Sculptors* says it all:

> *"And each agreed they would have failed If either had worked alone. For behind the parent stood the school And behind the teacher, the home."*
> Anonymous

TWO SCULPTORS

"I dreamed I saw a studio
And watched two sculptors there.
The clay they used was a child's mind
And they fashioned it with care.

One was a teacher - the tools he used
Were books, music and art.
The other, a parent, worked with a guiding hand,
And a gentle, loving heart.

Day after day, the teacher toiled with
touch that was careful, deft, and sure.
While the parent labored by his side
And polished and smoothed it o'er.

And when at last, their task was done,
They were proud of what they had wrought.
For the things they had molded into the child
Could neither be sold nor bought.

And each agreed they would have failed
If either had worked alone.
For behind the parent stood the school
And behind the teacher, the home."

– Anonymous

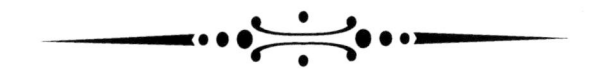

"The best and most beautiful things in the world cannot be seen, nor touched. . .but are felt in the heart."

HELEN KELLER

CHAPTER 9

Creating Intimacy and Fostering Self-Esteem Through Storytelling

The first time that I can recall ever being excited about hearing a story was when I was a little girl of five or six years old. It was told by my favorite television star at the time, Shari Lewis and her puppets Lambchop, Charlie Horse and Hush Puppy.

Shari used each of her puppets as characters in her tale. The way she changed her voice to fit the characters, the excitement in her eyes, and the manner in which she narrated the story made the dialogue come alive right before me. I was hooked by the whole experience. My family room had become transformed into a little theater, and I was connected by that *intimacy link* which enabled me to feel a true catharsis for all the puppets on stage.

Shari Lewis became my role model. I wanted to tell stories the way she did. I wasn't a trained ventriloquist, but I sure loved using different voices, working the puppets and singing songs. At a very young age I was bitten by the storytelling bug. It has lasted ever since.

As it turns out, my very favorite thing to do with my class is to tell stories. It doesn't matter whether I read them, make them up, or share stories from my childhood or present day life. What does matter is that every story I tell is told with tremendous enthusiasm and an awareness of how my audience (my class) will receive it (an age appropriate engaging tale).

My stories come alive. I marinate my students in all the flavors of the tale, emphasizing the characters, setting, beginning, middle and ending. By doing so, I draw a picture in their minds that is so vivid that they feel as though they are on a trip with me and have left school behind.

"The single most important activity for building the knowledge required for eventual success in reading is reading aloud to children."
Anderson, Heibert, Wilkinson, 1985

For this assignment, I asked my first grade students to draw a picture of how they felt when I read a story to them. As you can see, in Kayla's drawing there I am reading a story about what it would be like if we lived in the dinosaur era. Kayla drew a picture of me reading the story. She is sitting on the *Magic Carpet* with her classmates, listening to it attentively.

I asked Kayla to tell about what she drew above herself. She said, "Ms. Lipper, that is my thinking bubble. I was thinking about what it would have been like to have lived with the dinosaurs. Maybe one would have been my friend!"

After reading a story, there were times when I would engage the children in conversation regarding the sequence of events in the book. Many times I would stop at a crucial part in the book and have the students predict how the story might end.

Telling a wonderful story can serve as a catalyst for so many activities. Using their imaginations, I have had my students do these activities at different times:

- Draw a picture of their *favorite part* of the story. Write about it when possible.

- Draw a picture of their *favorite character* in the story. Write about him or them.

- Change the story's ending, and draw a picture of the *new ending*. Write about it.

- Fold your large paper in thirds and *draw a scene* from the *beginning, middle,* and *end* of

Nuturing Our Children To Succeed **89**

the story. Write a sentence or two describing each part.

- Design *stick puppets* for the characters of the story. Retell the story.

- Create a *paper bag puppet* of your favorite character.

- Make *masks* with a few friends and act out the story.

- Create *clay character figures*.

All writing activities are done when the children have begun using inventive spelling and are ready.

My first grade classroom became a small theater one day when I read and acted out the story of "*Brave Irene*" by William Steig. I reenacted Irene's daring trip through a snowstorm, carrying a dress that her mother had made for the princess. I wrapped one of my dresses in a large box, got dressed in my winter clothes, and read the story as though the blizzard was about to whirl me across the classroom. When I got to the end, my students cheered and asked me if I'd read it again.

My classes always loved when I acted out the story of "*Cinderella*". Their favorite part was when the clock struck midnight and Cinderella ran off, leaving her glass slipper behind. It was my slipper flying across the back of the room that left them requesting that I read the story again.

When it was appropriate to our lesson, I would share a story from my childhood. My students got such a kick out of my adventures as a six or seven year old. One day we were talking about their pets, so I told them the true story of how we got our parakeet "Chippy." Chippy had flown into the living room through the window of my grandmother's sixth floor apartment. Again, I acted out this long adventure, that ended up with us keeping the parakeet and naming her Chippy. We never found the owner.

I told my students one Chippy story of how I woke up in the middle of the night when I was their age, to find Chippy sitting on top of the curtain rod in my bedroom. She had gotten out of her cage and flown upstairs.

There were many skills and activities that I was able to present from this story as a follow-up later on. For example, I was able to review the digraph *ch* for Chippy. We talked about other words that began with the same sound - *chicken, children, chalk, chew,* etc... We talked about the names of birds that are kept as pets and birds that we see flying outside in our neighborhood.

Regardless of whether I was reading one of my favorite childrens' books or whether I was retelling a true story from my childhood days, I was always aware of the great *intimacy link* that I could make with my audience if I could draw them into my love of storytelling.

Quite often, when I'd pick my students up from their weekly library class, they would be anxious to show me that they had checked out books that I had read to them at one time or another. Moreover, if it wasn't the same title as one of my previous selections, they were quick to point out that the book was written by one of my favorite authors.

When reading stories about famous people in American history, I would dramatize some aspect of the person's life, taking the children back in time and to another place. For example, after reading the biography of Martin Luther King, I pretended like I was Dr. King and I recited parts of the "I Have A Dream" speech, pretending I was in Washington, D.C. My students were mesmerized. They requested it over and over again.

We can plant the seeds for a love of reading and storytelling in our children's lives. All it takes is the desire to make it happen.

PART TWO

THE ROLE OF THE FAMILY IN HELPING OUR CHILDREN MEET SUCCESS IN SCHOOL

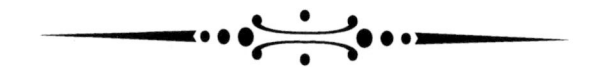

> *"Your children need your presence more than your presents."*
>
> — Jessie Jackson

CHAPTER 10

The Importance of Quality Family Time

With such scenarios as single-parent families, two parents holding full-time jobs, all different schedules among siblings, quality family time often seems to be at a minimum these days.

I was watching television the other night, when a commercial came on that peaked my interest. The camera focused in on an empty kitchen table and chairs as the actor said something that went like this: "Did you know that this is the most important place for you and your family to be? Spend time listening to your children! Make sure that the family *eats together* whenever possible. That's where some of the *most important* discussions take place!!" **BRAVO!! HOW TRUE!!**

What a public service this commercial is doing.

I am a firm believer, based on my years of listening to and spending time with young children, that quality family time can greatly contribute to a child's overall happiness and well-being in the home as well as in school. Over the years, parents have disclosed to me how badly they felt for not spending enough quality time with their children. They explained that because their schedules were so hectic, they were sometimes impatient and short-tempered with their own kids. By the time the weekend rolled around, they were too exhausted to really enjoy their precious moments with them.

This may, and often does, have a cumulative effect on a child, causing a child to feel hurt, unimportant, and even neglected. Unfortunately, those feelings can be carried with them to school, manifesting in different behaviors such as an inability to focus in on a task for some amount of time.

How can a child concentrate in school when he is very rarely required to interact and share his true self at home? They must encourage their child to read to them whenever possible. Why should a child be motivated to learn, if it seems that his parents aren't interested in what is going on in his life?

I will never forget what happened one day when I asked the students of one of my first grade classes to draw a picture of something that they liked to do with their father. (If they didn't have a father, they could draw a picture of something they liked to do with their grandpa, uncle, etc.) This drawing was going to be used for a book that we were making called *"My Family."*

I distributed the drawing paper, after modeling for the students some of the things I used to love to do with my dad as a child (i.e., go to the beach, a movie, the park, etc.) Everyone seemed to be very enthusiastic about the assignment except for Sally, who put her head down on the desk and began to cry. I happened to be walking past her desk, when she stood up and said, "Ms. Lipper, I don't want to do this! I can't do it!" With that, I put my hand on her shoulder and said, "You know what, let's walk over to my desk where we can talk privately." (My students knew that I would always be glad to speak to them privately about anything that was upsetting them.)

I pulled two chairs next to my desk. I sat on one and Sally sat on the other. "Can you please tell me why you don't want to do this?", I asked. With that, Sally responded, with tears streaming down her eyes, "There isn't anything that my daddy and I do together!" So, trying to help, I said, "There must be something that you and daddy do together that is fun." With that, she began to cry even more. "Ms. Lipper, you don't understand. My daddy works *all the time*! I never get to do anything with him." "What about on Saturdays and Sundays?", I asked. "He works on most of the weekends, he even has to travel, and then I don't see him for two weeks some times", she said.

Okay, by now I was feeling so badly for Sally. First, I validated her sadness by telling her how sorry I was that her father didn't spend enough time with her. Then, I asked her to think hard of a time when daddy didn't have to work so much. Her whole face lit up, and she said that she was going to draw a picture of when daddy took her skiing with the whole family up in Vermont. I asked her to tell me a little bit more about that trip. She explained that when she was four years old, the family spent Christmas vacation together in Vermont. She had the best time with her dad. He took her for skiing lessons, and they spent the entire week skiing and playing in the snow. I asked her if she felt better and was ready to work on her drawing. She said that she was okay, so she returned to her seat and began the task.

Sally's story further illustrates the importance of how my role as a teacher requires me to try my best at meeting the needs of all of my students.

From what happened in the classroom that day, I was able to form an important *intimacy link* with Sally through our emotional conversation. I also learned something critical concerning what Sally was feeling about her home life. The good news is that Sally drew a fantastic drawing of her trip to Vermont. I asked her if I could keep it, to show her parents at an upcoming conference. She was thrilled with the idea.

Shortly after, I called Sally's Mom and asked her if she and her husband would be able to attend the evening conference together. I explained to her that it would be most beneficial if I could speak to both of them about Sally's progress in school. We agreed on a time, and ultimately had an extremely productive talk.

At the conference, I let Sally's parents know what had transpired during the *family lesson* follow-up activity. I told them that it was very important that they got the full account of what happened so that they could help Sally continue to process her feelings concerning her father's work schedule.

They loved her drawing, and thanked me so much for taking the time with Sally. Sally's parents disclosed to me how important my feedback was for them. They knew that Sally missed her Dad. However, they didn't know that it was bothering her as much as it was.

Sally's Dad explained that his new job, as District Sales Representative for his company, required him to work long hours (in the beginning). However, he would be able to eventually delegate more responsibility to the individual sales representatives, and therefore work less overtime hours.

Sally's father said that he was going to make it his business to spend some true quality time with his daughter so that she wouldn't miss him so much. I told Sallys' parents how appreciative I was for their openness and willingness to help their daughter at home and in school.

We had a most productive conference, which was highlighted by another *intimacy link* between myself and Sally's mom and dad.

There are ways to create quality family time within a somewhat hectic life-style. It is so important to find activities to share with your child. Share your personal interests and passions with them. Your excitement will become contagious. At the same time, you can be discovering your child's interests and passions.

Here are just some of the many ideas for spending quality family time with your child:

- *Go to the park together.* (You were a kid once. PLAY!!! You will like it).

- *Go to a movie and talk about it afterward.* (I can still remember when my grandma took me to see Cinderella. I always tell my classes about it).

- *Go bowling.* (Explain how the game works. Teach your children the math).

- *Go bike riding together.*

- *Go to the beach.* Play in the waves, build sand castles, have a picnic.

- *Make a picnic.* Fly a kite, play ball, have a catch.

- *Go to* baseball games.

    soccer games.
                         [explain the rules]
    football games.

    basketball games.

- *Go to the zoo.* Teach your children all about the animals and their habitats. Make a book of the animals in the zoo.

- *Help your child start a collection* - sea shells, stamps, comic books, baseball cards, football cards, etc.

- *Take time for* ballet lessons, gymnastics, singing, guitar, piano, etc. Play instruments together, sing songs together.

- *Talk to your child* at the dinner table, in the car, on the way to school, after school, before they go to sleep, before they leave for school.

- *Go out for dinner.* It will give you a break once in a while from household chores.

- *Play indoor family games* - board games, Scrabble for Juniors, Monopoly for Juniors, Sorry, Boggle, etc., card games, checkers.

- *Visit a museum* - Museum of Natural History, Planetarium, Aquarium.

- *Family vacation* - Cooperstown, Washington, D.C., Disneyland, Camping.

- *Make family photo albums.* Show your child how to use a simple disposable camera. Take pictures of family time, special events, holidays, etc. Write a little paragraph describing the time. Date it. It will last for a lifetime.

Spend meaningful time with your child! I guarantee you that when your children grow up, they will always look back with fond memories on the quality family times that they shared with you.

In the following assignment, I asked one of my former students to draw a picture of something she liked to do with her sister.

She drew a picture of herself and her sister Susan talking in the TV room. She said, "It helps us feel better when we're stuck in a situation or when we're sad or annoyed. It feels so nice to know that I have someone to talk to when I'm mad, sad or feeling blue."

For the following exercise, I asked one of my former students to draw a picture of something she liked to do with her mother or father.

She drew a picture of herself and her family traveling to Virginia. She said, "I love my family. I like to go to Virginia because I get to see my cousins and get to go to the water parks."

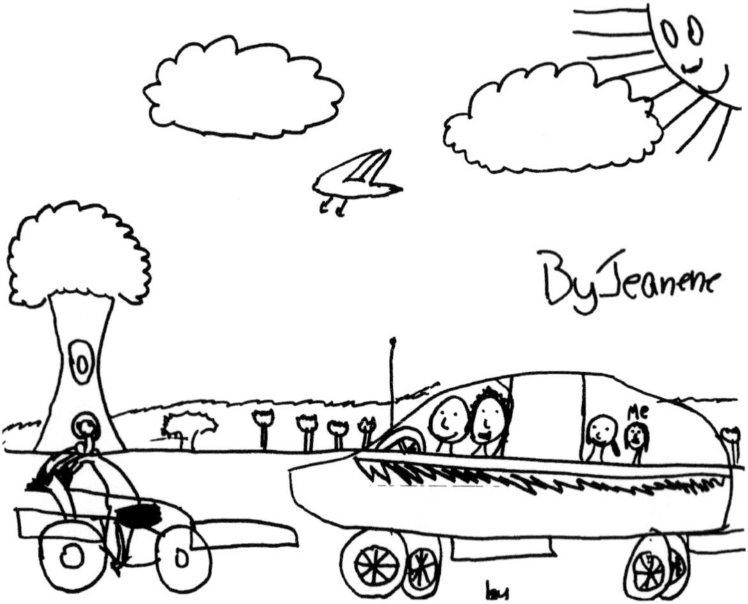
By Jeanene
me

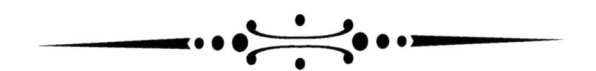

> "*I can live two months on a good compliment.*"
>
> — MARK TWAIN

CHAPTER 11

Suggestions For Parents On Establishing Healthy Communication That Will Enhance Their Child's Self-Esteem

Did you know studies have shown that, in general, for every positive message a child gets during the day, there are at least four negative ones received? *Unfortunately, some adults, parents and/or teachers are not always aware of the type of message they are sending to a child. All too often, they do not focus enough on the positive behavior that a child demonstrates. They are too quick to criticize and forget the importance of praise.*

Pertaining to this very topic, I will never forget a conference that I had with a parent of a first grader a few years ago. I asked her son to please bring over his handwriting book from his desk so that he could show his mom how much improvement he had made in forming his letters.

After he spent two minutes trying to locate the books from somewhere in his desk, his mother, without seeming to have any concern as to how I would react to this interaction with her son, shouted across the room, "It figures! Randi is so lazy. He's such a mess! He can never find anything. Ms. Lipper, he's the same way at home!"

"Wow!" Now the pieces of the puzzle were starting to come together. No wonder Randi looked down at the floor when he spoke to me. Moreover, whenever it came to speaking within the classroom setting, especially participating in a lesson, he seemed to lack confidence when responding. Randi was probably being bombarded with negative messages at home.

I knew that I could model good communication for Randi's mom, and I also wanted her to see what negative messages she was giving Randi. So, I told her that Randi was a very hard worker. I told Randi that I would help him organize his desk. I said that when I was a little girl I remember feeling overwhelmed with all the stuff that I had to keep in my desk. Sometimes I would feel badly when I couldn't find an item. It happens to a lot of us.

If you consistently give your child negative messages, these negative messages will become their truth. Your opinion of them, your judgements of their behavior and style are what will greatly contribute to defining how they see themselves within the context of the outside world.

How you judge them is how they will judge themselves!!

> *"Many children are reluctant to bring their thoughts and feelings to our attention because they believe that if they are honest and open, we will be shocked or angry. Children often do not think and feel as we expect them to, or as we think they should, but it is always inappropriate for us to punish them for their thoughts or feelings. We may have to acquire new skills in listening and accepting what they say."*
>
> Apter, Ph.D., 1997

Children take what you say so strongly. *They internalize your message because you are the most important people in their lives.* If, throughout their childhood, you give them consistent messages that you believe in them and love them unconditionally, you will have given them one of the most cherished gifts toward achieving successful, happy adult lives.

There are subtle ways that we as teachers and parents can act that will contribute to enhancing a child's self-esteem.

At times, we are unaware of the often negative ramifications of some of our behaviors. For instance, the tone in which we talk to our children may contribute towards good communication with them. On the other hand, if they are often addressed in a harsh tone, they may ultimately shut down, feel unloved, and constantly criticized.

Throughout my career I have tried my best to use a gentle, soft tone when addressing my students. Of course, if a situation warranted a voice change, I would have to speak in a firm tone, and increase the volume of my message. Once my students spent a few days with me, they trusted that I would treat them gently and with respect.

Some children are very sensitive to an adult's facial expressions. If you regularly look at a child as if she's done something wrong or has greatly disappointed you, she will not have faith in your feelings for her.

I am a strong proponent for showing your child affection. *Be demonstrative.*

Demonstrate to your child how authentic your love is by modeling kindness in the home. Be kind and gentle with your children, and they will trust your love.

I am a strong believer in telling your child how much you love him as often as possible. Children need to feel comforted. Every child needs hugs, kisses and endearing messages. No matter how hectic your life might be, send your children off to school with a positive message and greet them with love, no matter how difficult your day was. Save that special place for them, and they will never forget your kindness.

One of my favorite things that I have said to my nephew since he could first comprehend language was "Do you know how much I love you?" With that, he'll look at me, opening his big brown eyes so brightly and say, "How much?" I'll grab him in my arms, kiss his cheeks, and say *MORE THAN ALL THE HOT STARS IN THE SKY*!!"

Let your children know how much they mean to you. Every year, since I started teaching, I make the time to tell my students how special they are. I compliment them whenever possible. I always take the time to tell each class how much I love them. I set the tone for a positive, productive environment.

Over the years I have seen parents write such loving notes to their children. They often put them on a post-it with their snacks or lunch. This lets the child know that his parent loves him and is thinking about him during the day.

As I discussed in Chapter 10, spending quality time with your child is very important. It will contribute to making your child feel good about himself.

For this activity, I asked a former student of mine to draw a picture of something his mom or dad does or says that makes him feel good about himself. He said that "I like when my dad takes me to Shea Stadium. I love to spend time with him."

Nuturing Our Children To Succeed **113**

My Dad takes me to Shea to see the New York Mets. I love to spend time with him.

By Robert

As children get older, they become increasingly aware of the issues affecting them, their families, and the world. We must keep the lines of communication open. It is our responsibility to be sensitive to their needs and worries.

For this drawing, I asked one of my former students, who was going to be graduating in June, what she worries about. She said that she was afraid of growing up. She was afraid that she would start to change in many ways.

Praise your childs' efforts and let them know that you are aware of how hard things are for them at times. Let them know that you were once a child. Recognize their unique style and find the beauty in it. Let them go at their own pace. Allow them their individuality and encourage it.

Listen to your children today. Don't wait for tomorrow. Let them speak their truth and hopefully you will have a healthy, authentic relationship with them for years to come.

I know that in our over stressed lives it can be very difficult at times to nurture ourselves, let alone our children.

Children require your stamina and patience, as well as your love. Enlisting the help of grandparents can provide love and nurturing for your children especially during the times when you are feeling overwhelmed with lifes' demands.

by: Shahira

Now · Later

I'm afird of growing up because I will start to change in many ways which I don't want to happen to me.

A patient, kind grandma or grandpa will be terrific company for your child and will afford you the opportunity to decompress at the same time.

Some of the most endearing intimacy links are formed between Grandparents and their Grandchildren further enhancing a child's self-esteem.

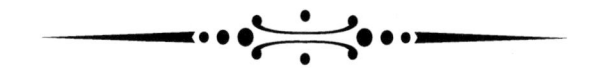

"Literature is my utopia."

HELEN KELLER

CHAPTER 12

READ! READ! READ!

In Chapter 9, I talked about how much I loved reading and storytelling with my students.

In this chapter, I will further emphasize the importance of reading to your child *at home* on a regular basis. Not only is it important to read to your child, it is equally important to listen to your child as he or she begins to read.

Even if it's only for fifteen minutes at the end of a long day, have your child read a page from his reading book, and you can start to read a story and continue it the next night. The books should be age appropriate. (Funny and light is always a big hit at bedtime). This completes the day on a happy note, and can be the start of some sweet dreams to come.

Share your love for reading with your children. Children model after what they see at home. You can be the catalyst for building your child's home library. Books will bring inner joy for the whole family. Discuss the stories that interested and excited you as a child. Your children will live vicariously through your strong emotions around books.

It seems like yesterday that I was sitting beside my dad on the couch in our family room, surrounded by shelves of books covering topics from Art and History to Science Fiction. Actually, I was probably about eight years old at the time. I can't remember the title of the book, nor do I recall our discussion that afternoon. However, I do cherish the memory of the special experiences of being in my father's favorite place and sharing his love for reading with him.

My dad was a voracious reader. Everywhere he went you'd find a book by his side. I remember wondering as a child, if my father was a genius. His vocabulary was so extensive and his knowledge on all kinds of subject matter never ceased to amaze me. My father's unique love for reading was catching. He was a tremendous role model for me. I wanted to find out what was inside these books. What made them so special that he couldn't put them down? Reading was his passion, and so it became mine.

On a somewhat sadder note, my father carried the love of learning with him until he could not learn any more. On the day that he died, there beside him was his latest book. It was opened to the page that he had been reading. This was the final chapter of his life, but there were probably millions of chapters that came before it.

You might be asking yourself, "What does this have to do with my child?" That's just it. Within this glimpse of my life is the universal theme that *children model after what they see at home.* Be a good role model for your children. READ! READ! READ!

For the following assignment, I asked a former student of mine to draw a scene from his favorite book. He drew a scene from "The Black Cauldron." He said that he liked this story because it was a big adventure about a boy who wanted to become a knight. He then told me that he really loved it because he felt like he was in it.

By reading this tale, Nicholas was able to journey to a make believe place.

Nuturing Our Children To Succeed 121

THE BLACK Cauldron

BY: NICHOLAS

One day last year I asked my first graders to draw a picture of how they felt when their mother or father read to them. Corrie told me that she felt so happy when her mom read her a story.

An additional way for spending quality family time as discussed in Chapter 10 would be taking a trip to the children's section of the public library. Let your child take part in the process of selecting a book. Spend some time at the library during the summer months. Find out what programs are being offered. Encourage your child to participate.

Help your child to become interested in the written language of her environment. What signs can your child recognize on the road, storefronts, trucks, restaurants, gas stations, food labels, etc.?

When watching television together, encourage him to try to identify words (i.e., names of products, shows, public service messages, etc.)

Start a word bank together out of a milk container. Cover the container and make it into a story-book character. Put in small word cards with the new words your child is able to recognize and/or read. Every now and then empty the bank and praise your child for learning so many new words.

Nuturing Our Children To Succeed **123**

Corrie   June 9, 1998

My mom is reading a stroy. And I am happy.

Select a few stimulating childrens' educational programs on television and watch them with your child. You can emphasize the reading skills highlighted on the show. There are truly endless opportunities out there for parents to share their love of reading with their children.

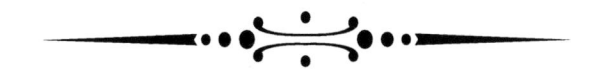

"Your involvement can help to further strengthen that intimacy link, if you treat your children gently and give them positive messages concerning their efforts."

SUSAN LIPPER

CHAPTER 13

Homework Doesn't Have To Be A Big Struggle

I remember my friends and I cheering during the days in elementary school when my teachers announced "NO HOMEWORK TONIGHT!"

What was it about homework that drove most of us crazy at times? We prayed for the substitute teacher because it usually meant no homework that night unless otherwise specified.

How many of us wanted to sit down and do homework after a long day of school? Let's face it, very few of us really enjoyed one more academic task on our plates. We had had enough.

As the school bus approached my bus stop, I can recall gazing out the window, going into an end of the day trance, and fantasizing about the delicious snacks that would await me at home before I'd go out to play with my friends.

Looking back on that time, I guess I didn't actually realize how lucky I was to have had a mom who understood that because of my style of learning, I needed some time to decompress before I could approach any school related activity.

So, when my friends rang my doorbell and asked if I could go outside, I very rarely heard those ghastly words, "not until she finishes her homework!"

Oh boy! How would you like to be welcomed like that as you walked through the door after a long day of work! I know I certainly wouldn't. I would not want to address one more work related task.

It's very important for us as adults to empathize with our children whenever possible. Each one of them has their own unique learning style. True, there are always those students who will want to do their homework right after school. However, I can assure you that they are the minority.

Students who are not given a choice as to when they can do their homework will eventually end up in a power struggle with a parent, often resenting them and dreading the mere thought of the required daily assignment and the word HOMEWORK.

I realize that parents' schedules can sometimes conflict with homework demands. However, if you want homework to be a healthy learning experience for your child, you must try to be as flexible as possible.

What seems to work in many families, and how my mom addressed my homework time as a child was: 1) come home; 2) have a snack; 3) play inside or out; 4) do your homework; 5) have dinner (or have dinner and then do your homework).

Whichever scenario perpetuates a healthy attitude towards homework is what will best serve your childs' needs in the long run.

At the kindergarten and first grade level it is okay in the beginning of the school year to help your child locate the assignment in his schoolbag, review what is required, and guide your child if needed, without doing the task for him.

Your involvement can help to further strengthen that *intimacy link* if you treat your child gently and give him positive messages concerning his efforts. In time, you should see your child develop a more independent attitude toward doing his homework.

As the year progresses, if the homework is appropriately reviewed in school, your child should be working more independently, requiring less direction and help from you.

However, if you often notice that he is becoming discouraged and frustrated with the task and he almost always needs a lot of help from you in completing it, then it would be most advantageous for you to call his teacher and explain the difficulty, either on the telephone or at a future conference.

On a lighter note, over the years I have seen a few unsightly homeworks returned to me. There were a number of times when I distributed a clean worksheet to a student, and got back a homework assignment that looked as if it had fallen in a plate of spaghetti, or had been crumpled for deposit in the trash can, or was trampled on by the family dog. Alright, you got the message.

Please impress upon your child the need to do her homework in a quiet (no TV), clean area, with good lighting. Establishing a good homework routine will help your child develop the proper work and study habits for the future.

By the way, if you don't understand what's required for an assignment, and your child can't explain it either, there may be something wrong. Remember, **even teachers make mistakes!!** Send it to school the next day with your child. Attach a little note explaining that you don't understand what to do. (This will relieve your child of any possible anxiety concerning the homework).

When homework is based on material presented in class that day, or material that was previously taught, it can reinforce skills and leave the child with a sense of accomplishment.

It amazed me when a first grade child approached me the morning after I gave out a homework assignment and said something like this: "Ms. Lipper, I am so sorry. Please don't be mad. My mommy had an appointment last night and we got home late. I didn't get to do the homework! I promise I'll do it tomorrow." I hadn't even had the chance to see who submitted their work yet. The student was being so honest and responsible. Usually, I would use my sense of humor, which they were all too familiar with, and say, "All right, then you'll have to do six homeworks tonight to make up for it!" With a big smile across their face, they'd say, "Oh, Ms. Lipper! You are so silly!" I'd give them a big hug and say, "Don't worry about it. You can either work on it in class, or finish it at home whenever you get a chance."

I have never, ever, over my entire career, had trouble getting children to do their homework. (Unless there were extenuating circumstances interfering with the child's ability to do it, i.e., a learning disability, crises at home, etc.)

Homework doesn't have to be a big struggle!!

Believe it or not, there have been times (over a vacation break, weekends, holidays) when my students have requested homework when it wasn't required of them. I can't remember ever doing that. Can you?

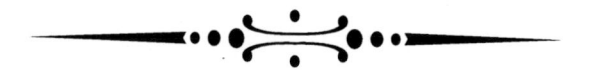

> *"I believe that this neglected, wounded, inner child of the past is the major source of human misery."*
>
> — JOHN BRADSHAW

CHAPTER 14

Informing Children About The Dangers In Our Society

The other day I walked into a busy local coffee shop, and as I approached the counter a little girl tapped me on the leg and said, "Do you like my costume? I am a clown." I said that I loved it, and proceeded to get on line behind her mom, who was ordering a cup of coffee for herself and an ice cream for her daughter.

We continued our conversation. "How old are you?", I asked. "I am four years old. I just came from my friend Annie's birthday party. We had to dress up in costumes", she said. With that, her mom turned to me and said, "It looks like she's going to tell you her whole life story." "That's okay", I said. "She's so adorable and she's such a happy, enthusiastic, articulate little girl. I love talking to her. However, it doesn't seem like she's afraid of strangers." Well, Vicki heard her mom and me talking about strangers, and all of a sudden looked up at me and asked, **"Are you a stranger?"** Before I could respond, Vicki's mom said, "It's okay to talk to this lady because mommy is with you. But, when you are by yourself, you shouldn't talk to anyone even if they seem nice. This lady started out as a stranger, but mommy was with you and I saw that this lady was kind. She's a teacher." (We had spoken about my career). "So, now it's okay to speak to her."

Vicki's mom and I talked about how difficult this concept can be for children at such a young age. You have to impress upon them the reality that there are people in the world who are not kind, even mean and dangerous. However, you don't want to alarm them so much that they become afraid of all adults in general.

In school we act out scenarios showing how a stranger can behave kindly toward a child in order to lure him into a dangerous situation. The motto is absolutely, positively, ***"DON'T TALK TO STRANGERS!"*** We tell our students that if a stranger approaches them at any time and for any reason, they should scream and run away immediately and then tell a close friend or family member (whoever they see first).

We as educators have a responsibility for making our students aware of the dangers in our society. In the early grades we educate our children as to the dangers of smoking cigarettes, using alcohol and drugs, to not wearing automobile seatbelts, talking to strangers, unsafe outdoor play, playing with matches, and physical and sexual abuse, etc.

Unfortunately, in today's society, on a regular basis, children may hear reports of other children being kidnapped, sexually assaulted, and/or murdered. They often see real pictures on their television screens of adults being held up at knife point or gun point and being killed for a measly few dollars.

All across our newspaper pages, children have been exposed to a host of cruelties. Some of the ones that received the greatest amounts of attention were the most recent school shootings in middle and high schools located in different parts of our country. Can you imagine how frightened a kindergartner or first grader might feel returning to school after learning that these children were murdered by other children. Their fellow classmates no less! What emotional scars will this image leave on little kids? Will they become nervous in their own class? Will they worry that guns will go off in the next school they attend? The possible negative future emotional consequences of the intensity of these events and the impact they might have on children in general, and the younger child in particular, is something that remains to be seen.

Unfortunately, I can recall many instances when I have had to instill a sense of calm in the hearts and minds of my students pertaining to a tragic incident that they had heard of from another person or had seen on the news. Often, children are so alarmed by the images of a horrific event that it's the first thing that they talk about when they arrive at school.

There have been additional very visible acts of violence that children have been exposed to in recent years. The following are some of the most catastrophic: terrorist bombings in Northern Ireland, the Middle East, the Gulf War, the War in Kosovo and Bosnia, (the horrific effects of land mines), the O.J. Simpson trial (murders of Nicole Simpson and Ron Goldman), the senseless, cruel stabbing of Monica Selles - the outstanding tennis player and her loss of innocence at such a young age.

The following were some events that occurred in locations closer to the students in my school: the World Trade Center bombing, Pan Am flight number 103 bombing, TWA flight number 800 crash off Long Island, and the one that hit closest to home was the Long Island Railroad massacre where a train full of innocent people left their homes for what they thought would be an ordinary day of work, to be confronted by a deranged mass murderer. The father of one of my former kindergarten students was murdered aboard that train.

How do we begin to explain these horrific events to our children?

Unfortunately, most of the time there is no explanation for a senseless, barbaric act of violence.

However, we as teachers and parents must be sensitive to our children, and take the time to put them at ease as much as possible. Talk to them about their fears on a level that they can understand and try not to be over protective. Unfortunately, being overprotective could be keeping a child form experiencing confidence and independence in the outside world.

> *"Our children will be far more likely to find us guilty of excessive caution than they are to appreciate our reasonable care. The best we can do is continue to pit our assessment of danger against our children's need to have their judgment and independence encouraged."*
> Apter, Ph.D., 1997

Parents must be hypervigilant with supervising any television images that your children might view. There is a great need for parents to monitor and select the programs watched by their kids. Children are extremely impressionable at five, six or seven years old, and may have a hard time differentiating between fantasy and reality.

Studies have shown that young children who hear violent language and witness violent behavior on television, on a regular basis, may experience a high level of anxiety regarding their own safety in the world.

Young children should **never** play or be exposed to violent video games.

Try your best to watch the news only after your child has fallen asleep. Television news can frighten young viewers to the point where they might have difficulty falling asleep. These disturbing images can often cause nightmares.

We must establish a sense of security for our children by reassuring them that they are safe at home. We can do that by discussing and emphasizing the happy events that occur during the week (i.e., the Mets won another game, we have cousin Bonnie's birthday party, etc.).

In our schools we must elect to have more programs focused on character building, and conflict resolution starting at the elementary level so that children learn to address and appropriately deal with their problems at a very young age. We must allocate additional funding for more mental health professionals to be hired in our elementary, middle and high schools.

WE MUST NOT WAIT until a twelve year old is caught with a knife, or a fifteen year old fires a loaded shotgun and kills his fellow classmates.

How and why did this happen again? —The tragic massacre at Columbine High school, a suburb outside of Denver, Colorado. What were all the variables that contributed to two high school students opening fire and exploding pipe bombs on an entire population of their teachers and peers?

The victims could have been any one of our Children!!!

Changes must take place now, from Pre-K on up!

From what we now know of this horrific, senseless act of violence, no one variable acted in isolation to detonate the hearts of those teenage boys filled with mountains of hatred. It was clearly a combination of factors that contributed to this mayhem.

Guns must be **eliminated** from the hands of our children. Anger can never, ever go unchecked, unnoticed, and/or unaddressed.

We as individual adults can make a difference. If you know of a troubled child, a disenfranchised child, a child taking the wrong fork in the road, let your **voice** be **heard**!! Don't let anyone quiet it. Tell someone until this child gets help. Talk to a teacher, a parent, a clergyman, a principal, a counselor etc. And follow-up on what was done regarding this child's situation.

We as principals, teachers, and parents must take any warning signs of future violence seriously. First and foremost, all of us in the community of adults must be role models for our children.

> *"In most cases, teenagers who are aggressive or violent, show anti-social behavior early in life. If they don't get help early, they continue to become more aggressive. Some eventually become violent. On the other hand, we also know that when children can connect with adults who are good role models - whether at home, in school or in the community - they are less likely to become aggressive or violent."*
>
> Gorman, 1998.

I will never forget what happened one day as I was taking one of my first grade classes in from the schoolyard. I called back to our door monitor to close the door behind her. With that, I heard one of my students yell out, "You heard her, you idiot, shut the DAMN door!" I couldn't believe my ears. I had never heard a six year old talk that way (especially in our school). So, I stopped the class and quickly asked that student to come up and talk to me privately on the side. Not really thinking in reaction to what he said, I asked, "Did you ever hear me call someone an *idiot* and use the word *damn*?" Right at that moment he looked at me with such an expression of sincerity and said, "No, Ms. Lipper, but my father says shut the *damn* door all the time when we let our cat out, and he calls me an idiot all the time when I do the wrong thing."

Well, now all the pieces of the puzzle had fit together. This was the way he was spoken to at home.

Speak to your children with *love*! Be aware of the messages you send. You owe it to your child.

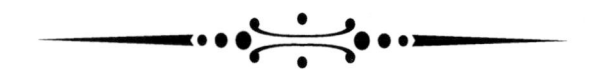

"Hope is the thing with feathers that perches in the soul - and sings the tune without words and never stops - at all."

Emily Dickinson

CHAPTER 15

A Positive Vision For the Future

Reading the newspaper, listening to the radio, and watching the evening news on television serves as a constant reminder to me of how fragile all of our adult lives can sometimes feel. Can you imagine then, how vulnerable and frightened children must feel at times?

Even though our society continues to be plagued by many variables that can and often do interfere with the healthy emotional and academic development of our younger students, the good news is that I am optimistic and am holding onto my dream for a brighter tomorrow.

I believe that the recent focus by our president and governors on putting a stop to the unacceptable, horrific violence in many of our schools has led to a healthy dialogue concerning all the major factors facing our students today. Our national consciousness has been raised, hopefully for good, on the urgent need to improve the schools throughout our country.

I have spent over two decades observing and experiencing firsthand the ways in which a *nurturing classroom environment* can act as a stabilizing and motivating force in a child's life.

From Pre-K on, parents and teachers working together with respect, trust and ultimately even love for each other, can make a great impact on the child's development at home and in school. As partners, working toward the common goal of helping the child become a more self-motivated, confident student, they can serve as healthy role models for the child's future years.

For the following exercise, I asked a former student of mine to draw a picture of how she would like the world to be. She said, "Ms. Lipper, I'd like the sun to shine brightly on everyone. There would be no more violence and wars. Our world would be clean."

Let's work together to make a better world for our children.

In order to nurture our children to succeed in the early childhood grades, we need smaller classes with full-time educational assistants. There must

Nuturing Our Children To Succeed   145

Bad and Polluted

Good and Perfect   By Mallory

be ongoing programs for children in crisis run by sensitive mental health professionals.

It is mandatory that the school social workers and psychologists conduct workshops for teachers and parents concerning the ever increasing social and emotional challenges facing our students.

We need after school programs for the children of working parents, and children in need of remediation as well.

Teachers need to be made to feel safe when expressing their classroom needs to their principal. The teachers' concerns and recommendations must be investigated and acted upon in order for improvements to take place. Principals must schedule talks on a regular basis with their teachers regarding all sorts of issues that arise within the academic setting.

They must serve as role models for their staff, facing the truth in every volatile situation with courage and determination. *A teacher must never be forced to stand alone.*

I believe it can all be done. We are all connected by the love for our children. The cumulative effects of nurturing our children to succeed cannot be measured by statistical data.

However, they will be undeniably felt in the hearts and minds of our future generations to come.

I have shared my story with you because I know that my classroom is an exciting place. Through my creativity, sense of humor, sensitivity, and use of inspiring materials, I have consistently lit the fire of enthusiasm within the minds of my students.

As I stood in front of them, I could see their eyes widening and their hands raised with the energy of knowledge and confidence. It is one of the greatest pleasures a teacher can experience. My students were fully engaged in their learning. I had taken them by the hand and led them through a journey filled with the love of the subject which I had introduced at any given moment.

Our society is more than ready to launch a rocket toward educational growth for all of our children. So, establish an **intimacy link** with your child or student today. You will be happy you did.

Ten Steps To Nurturing Our Children To Succeed

(Of course, there's no set order)

- If you notice that your child doesn't seem herself, *ask* "Is everything all right?" ***"Can I help you with something?"*** "How was school today?" etc.

- ***Respect*** and ***validate*** your child's feelings whenever possible.

- ***Establish an intimacy link*** with your child. Speak in a gentle tone. Be aware of the message your eyes relay. Be physically demonstrative whenever possible. Tuck your child in at night. Gentle touch, and hugs are very healing. Hug and kiss your child before he leaves for school. Use the words "I Love You".

- Never hesitate to ***say you're sorry*** if the situation warrants it. They will never forget it.

- Let them know that ***you were once a kid***. You know how tough things can seem sometimes. Tell them your own personal stories from childhood.

- **Spend quality time with your child** and help them in a gentle manner. Use humor whenever possible. Have fun. Play! Laugh! Sing in the car!

- **Limit critical remarks** to a minimum. Remember to use **praise when appropriate**, congratulate, reward with a little something, get excited, show enthusiasm.

- **Be a positive role model** in the things you *say* and *do*. Your behavior will speak for itself.

- **Practice acts of kindness** at home and in the community. Get involved. Get your child involved.

- **Encourage risk taking!** (If you follow all the previous tips, the risk taking should come naturally).

NEED MORE HELP THAN YOUR SCHOOL CAN PROVIDE?

Sometimes more extensive support services are needed than what our schools can provide.

You can just imagine the intense grief of a young child over the loss of a parent, sibling, grandparent or close friend.

Too often grieving children don't have an outlet to express their tremendous pain.

Recently I saw a television show that highlighted an outstanding outreach program. It is called *Mary's Place*. This program, located in Connecticut, is actually a center for grieving families.

Therapists trained in the field of bereavement counseling, encourage the children to take part in activities that will enable them to share their feelings with other children who are in similar situations.

Three such activities greatly impressed me. The first one encouraged the children to express their feelings out loud and in front of the rest of the group by focusing on a prop called the *Talking Stick*. This colorful stick was passed around the group. When a child wanted to express his feelings he took the *Talking Stick*, held it in his hand and shared his sadness with his peers. His attention was diverted to the stick enabling him to disclose his pain instead of keeping it bottled up inside.

For the second activity children drew pictures or wrote something special to put on a *Memory Tree* depicting a special memory of their deceased family member.

Also displayed on a bulletin board was a beautiful drawing of another tree called the *Worry Tree*. The children drew pictures or wrote about something that worried them. (Often after a parent or sibling dies the child is worried that their other parent or sibling might die.) Each child placed his final product on a tree branch.

These were just three of the very meaningful, beautifully created activities that are used to help ease the pain of children in crisis.

It would be advantageous to look into what your community has to offer. Your children can benefit from as much support as possible. Many schools have on file updated lists of outreach programs that cater to the needs of our children. The following is a list of some of the types of programs available in communities throughout our country:

- Church and Synagogue programs.
- Youth Center programs.
- Community and/or settlement house programs for youth.
- Counseling centers.
- Hospital outreach programs.
- The Police Athletic League Programs.
- Mentor Programs such as Big Brothers and Big Sisters.
- Volunteer Organization Programs.
- Support Groups.
- Library Programs - lectures, workshops, etc.
- Youth Organizations
- Government Programs - County, City, State and Federal
- Corporate Responsibility Programs
- Social and Human Services Organizations
- Crisis Hotlines
- Foster Grandparents Program
- Anti-Defamation Outreach Programs

Bibliography

Anderson, Richard C., Heibert, Elfrieda H., Scott, Judith A., Wilkinson, G., "Becoming a Nation of Readers", in The Report of the Commission on Reading, Champain-Urbana, I., Center for the Study of Reading, 1985.

Apter, Terri, *The Confident Child*, New York: W.W. Norton, 1997.

Furstenberg, Frank and Cherlin, Andrew, *Divided Families: What Happens to Children When Parents Part?* Cambridge, MA.: Harvard University Press, 1991.

Ginott, Haim, *Teacher and Child*, New York: Macmillan, 1972.

Gorman, Trish, "The Warning Signs of Violent Behavior" in The American Teacher, Washington, D.C., Dec. 98/Jan. 99.

Healy, J.M., *Your Child's Growing Mind: A Parents' Guide to Learning*: N.Y. Doubleday, 1987.

Loomans, Diane, *Full Esteem Ahead*, Tiburon, California: H.J. Kramer Inc., 1994.

Marshall, Melinda, "Nurturing the Power of Make Believe" in Parenting: N.Y., Time Publishing Dec.'98/Jan.'99.

Middleton-Moz, Jane, *Children of Trauma*, Deerfield Beach, Fla.: Health Communications, 1989.

O'Gorman, P. and Oliver-Diaz, P., *Breaking the Cycle of Addiction*, Pompano Beach, Fla.: Health Communications, 1987.

Oliver, Carolyn and Bowler, Rosemary, *Learning to Learn*, N.Y.: Simon & Schuster, 1996.

Rich, D. *Mega Skills: How Families Can Help Children Succeed in School and Beyond*, Boston: Houghton, Mifflin, 1988.

Trelease, Jim, *The Read-Aloud Handbook*, New York: Penguin Books, 1979.

Weissbourd, Richard, *The Vulnerable Child*, Reading, MA.: Addison-Wesley, 1995.

About the Author

Susan Lipper has a Master's Degree in Elementary Education and has been teaching in the primary grades for over twenty years.

The majority of her teaching career has been spent in a middle-class school district comprised of students from multiethnic backgrounds where English is spoken as a second language in some of the homes. She is also licensed in teaching English as a Second Language.

Susan has always been very interested in the dynamics of the entire learning process. Throughout her career she has conducted workshops on *Creating Intimacy Through Storytelling*, *Reading Readiness*, *The Needs of E.S.L. Students*, S*elf-Esteem* and the *Elementary School Child*. Recently she developed a program on character building, called Practicing Acts of Kindness.

She has spoken in front of adult education classes, P.T.A. groups, faculty, and children throughout the grades.

Her message has always been that we must **connect and teach our children through laughter and love.**

To order additional copies of *Nurturing Our Children To Succeed* by mail, please send a check or money order for $17.45 ($14.95 plus $2.50 shipping) to:

    Susan Lipper
    90 S. Park Avenue
    Suite 8A
    Rockville Centre, NY 11570

❅ ❅ ❅ ❅ ❅ ❅ ❅ ❅ ❅ ❅ ❅ ❅ ❅ ❅ ❅ ❅ ❅

To order a cassette tape of *Nurturing Our Children To Succeed*, please send a check or money order for **$14.00 ($12.00 plus $2.00 shipping) to:**

    Susan Lipper
    90 S. Park Avenue
    Suite 8A
    Rockville Centre, NY 11570

❅ ❅ ❅ ❅ ❅ ❅ ❅ ❅ ❅ ❅ ❅ ❅ ❅ ❅ ❅ ❅ ❅

Susan Lipper is available to speak about her book *Nurturing Our Children To Succeed* and additional related topics.

Please call (516) 942-2015 to set up a workshop date and time.